Diversity in Day Care

—

Diversity in Day Care

Options
and
Issues

Rebecca Wheat, Ed.D.

TECHNOMIC
PUBLISHING CO., INC.
LANCASTER · BASEL

Published in the Western Hemisphere by
Technomic Publishing Company, Inc.
851 New Holland Avenue
Box 3535
Lancaster, Pennsylvania 17604 U.S.A.

Distributed in the Rest of the World by
Technomic Publishing AG

Printed in the United States of America
10   9   8   7   6   5   4   3   2   1

Main entry under title:
  Diversity in Day Care: Options and Issues

A Technomic Publishing Company book
Bibliography: p. 97

Library of Congress Card No. 88-50949
ISBN No. 87762-602-2

Table of Contents

v

Acknowledgements

This study was completed with the cooperation and support of many people. I would first like to thank my dissertation committee: Professor Emeritus Millie Almy, my advisor and chairperson; Professor Emeritus Kermit Wiltse; and Professor Sheila Walker. Professor Almy helped me immeasurably with the theoretical underpinnings of this study. Her continued support and infinite patience must be mentioned. Dr. Kermit Wiltse's inspiring course on day care generated many ideas which are incorporated in this study. Dr. Sheila Walker's courses on the use of methodology were invaluable to this work.

I am also grateful to Dr. Tony Stigliano and Dr. Paul Takagi for their excellent suggestions. I also wish to thank Karen Patterson for her indispensable help in typing this manuscript.

My warmest thanks to the families in the California community who shared their lives and their visions of day care with me and the day care directors who provided so many perspectives on day care.

Finally, I must thank my family—my husband Solomon and my children Derek and Caitlyn who have, throughout the course of this study, shown incredible love, patience, and support.

Introduction

Many of the people reading this book will reminisce about their own childhoods. In all likelihood their mothers were the "homemakers" and their fathers the "breadwinners." Men and women had clear, defined roles. Roles for children likewise were clear. In many ways there was an order and structure that created clarity and security.

In the past twenty-five years this world has been turned "upside down" (Yankelovich, 1981). The familiar has eroded and in its place we find new roles, new patterns, and new structures of family living. These new roles have generated changed expectations for men, women, and children.

Less than one-fifth of the families in the United States fit the "homemaker/breadwinner" family model. More than 60 percent of the mothers with children under fourteen are in the labor force, and approximately 50 percent of mothers are returning to work before their children turn one year of age (*Time,* June 1987).

It is now estimated that these figures will only escalate. In the year 2000, it is predicted that 80 percent of two-parent families will have both parents working, and there will be a 15.6 percent increase in the number of children under six (Blank, 1986).

The demands for child care are escalating and will continue to escalate. They have been precipitated by a myriad of factors: the changing roles of women and men; an increase in both divorce and single parenthood; smaller families with fewer grandparents, aunts, and cousins available for babysitting; and the changing economic picture which in many cases requires two incomes just to pay the rent, put food on the table, gas in the car, and clothes on the children.

Yankelovich has studied American trends for decades. He utilizes the term "giant plates of culture" (Yankelovich, 1981). The "plates of culture" alter the familiar. The landscape shifts and "huge dislocations" are created in our lives. Some feel the tremors more than others, but all are affected (Yankelovich, 1981). The "giant plates of culture" do not move backward but inexorably swing forward. It cannot be denied that the "Giant Plates of Culture" have swung forward. A study for the General Mills American Family Project of 1,230 families with children under six suggests that parents are less self-sacrificing than in previous years—less child-oriented and more self-centered (Yankelovich, 1976–77, cited in Clarke-Stewart, 1982).

As the plates of culture alter, we grapple with new patterns and structures to accommodate the altering plates. New patterns of caring for children become crucial as the work force changes, but new structures and supports in the care of America's children have lagged drastically behind the changing work force and the needs of our new work force.

Americans have historically seen the care of children as the province of the family, and day care has been associated with both welfare and deviancy. This negative connotation of child care, probably never accurate, certainly no longer fits America's families. Day care must be viewed in a positive light as a support for both our children and families. Unfortunately, the creation of excellent day care seems to be a very difficult task.

In the 1970s three child care bills (1971, 1975, 1979) were soundly defeated (Beck, 1982). Many politicians become wary of sponsoring child care legislation. Unfortunately, although the need for more child care is convincing, the individuals and groups promoting child care are splintered. Policy Analyst Rochelle Beck comments:

> Sometimes public policy is set by the sheer political strength of a particular interest. But in the case of child care, the diversity of groups, their difficulty in reaching consensus, and the emotion with which they express their views tend to confuse or

frighten policy-makers instead of encouraging them to make decisions. Unlike the lobbyists for the National Rifle Association, who speak out clearly on the issues, do not disagree among themselves in public, and represent an identifiable constituency that expresses itself politically and economically, those for child care are diffuse (Beck, p. 311).

At the same time that child care advocates are splintered, the opposition is consolidated, well-organized, and vociferous. They consistently hammer out the message that child care undermines the American family and basic American values (Beck, 1982).

Compared to other countries, America has a poor child care record. In Israel all five-year-olds attend school, as do 50 percent of the three- and four-year-olds, while Sweden boasts child development centers for 85 percent of the preschoolers and Hungary offers programs for half of its three- to six-year-olds (Zigler and Goodman, 1982). Unfortunately, what appears to be a right in other countries has become a privilege in the United States.

There is not a clear political force speaking for child care, and there is a lively debate within child care circles as to what types of child care should be offered. Should care be center-based or should family day care be promoted? What role should the family, the government, and the employer play in developing and financing child care?

Nowhere has the changing concept of child care been more altered than in the idea of employer-sponsored child care (Vezaro-O'Brien, 1986; Groser, 1986; Friedman, 1984). Employers can help with child care in many ways. Some employers have chosen to have on-site centers, but there are other ways employers can greatly help employees. Information about child care systems, flex-time, and financial assistance to cover all or part of child care costs are all options that can greatly support children and families (Friedman, 1984). Employers appear to benefit when supports for child care are given. Benefits include less job turnover, less absenteeism, and greater concentration at the job.

The trend in employer-sponsored child care is likely to continue. For instance, in the San Francisco Bay Area, Concord,

California, became the first city in the United States to require developer fees for child care. Developers of projects over $40,000 must provide child care on-site or pay 0.5 percent of the project's construction cost into a special fund allocated for child care (Brydolf, 1987). San Francisco, California, offers developers of commercial space of over 50,000 sq. ft. two options — pay a fee of $1.00 per sq. ft. or have space for child care (Brydolf, 1987).

Certainly any day care setting, whether at the school site or in the community, should interface with the needs of individual families. One way families can be offered a choice in day care settings is through the use of a voucher. The voucher can be offered through the employer or might come from various city or county governments or child care organizations. The voucher covers part or all of the child care costs and can be used at a variety of day care programs.

This book discusses one voucher experiment. Other experiments have also been conducted. The Phoenix Institute in Salt Lake City, Utah, studied families who utilized the voucher as an employer benefit (Clow, 1984). This successful program suggests that existing programs within the community should work together — public and private employers, parents, child care givers, real estate developers, and planners.

A large voucher project in New Jersey suggests that a voucher system can help parents become informed consumers, while at the same time, it increases a parent's access to quality child care (Catterall, 1985). The vouchering of child care suggests family choice and suggests the potential for a positive interface between home and child care and ultimately the hope that good quality child care can act as a positive support to families.

It is precisely this family-strengthening aspect of child care that must be articulated by the child care community. Good child care can enhance family functioning. Parents know that their children are being nurtured and well cared for during their working hours. When parents can pay, or are helped to pay, for high quality child care without putting a severe strain on their budgets, the whole society benefits.

High quality child development programs pay off. James Hymes notes that $1.00 spent in a child development program can lead to $4.75 of savings in special education and lower welfare costs (Hymes, 1987).

If we are to generate change in child care on a massive scale, it is imperative that new coalitions be formed. One coalition, the private–public coalition, is being successfully developed in the San Francisco Bay Area (Brydolf, 1987). The project, entitled the California Initiative, has helped add 1,200 day care slots. The foundation sought donations from large corporations and worked through the state's network of child care referral agencies which help parents find child care and assist child care providers in getting started. Between 1985 and 1986, more than 230 new day care providers were recruited and trained.

Another child care alliance is being developed by the prestigious National Association for the Education of Young Children (NAEYC). In a recent issue, the NAEYCs Public Policy Report discussed the creation of Alliance for Better Child Care (ABC) (May, 1987). Members are encouraged to institute a national effort to build support for child care. Letters have been sent to 300 national organizations involved with children and families, inviting their participation in the Alliance for Better Child Care (ABC).

The growth of quality child care will take alliances from public and private groups, working together in a unified way.

This book explores how one community has creatively solved some child care problems. The parents in this book have shared their ideas, hopes, concerns, and dreams and have articulately enriched our knowledge of child care issues.

As we enter the 21st Century, the way we care for our children and nurture our families should be a primary issue. May those committed to the very best child care rally together in support of the programs America's children truly deserve.

This study explores the relationship between parent values and the day care experience. It draws upon the day care literature and envelops this literature within the framework of human values. It employs open-ended interviews with both subsidized and non-subsidized day care parents as well as day care directors who have subsidized families in their programs.

The book is organized into themes and investigates the issue of subsidizing day care and how this relates to parental choice. Also explored are the issues of day care as a world of continuity or discontinuity, day care as an enriched or less than enriched world, and the relationship between day care and family life. The views of day care directors are also presented.

The research for this dissertation took place in a northern California community — a community which has a subsidized day care program. The dissertation is descriptive.

The Growing Need for Day Care

Care for the children of working mothers emerged as a critical issue in the 1970s. At that time, thirty percent of mothers with children under six years and with husbands present were in the labor force. Since then, the number of working mothers has steadily increased. By 1984, forty-eight percent of mothers with children under six years were in the labor force, as were nearly 50 percent of mothers with children under the age of one year. The Congressional Budget Office projects that by 1990, 55 percent of mothers with children under six years will be in the labor force (Miller, 1984). By 1990, the Bureau of Labor Statistics estimates that 66 percent of the individuals entering the work force will be women, and 80 percent of these women will be of childbearing age. Ninety-three percent of these women will become pregnant at some time during their work period (Miller, 1984). By the year 2000, 80 percent of two-parent families will have both spouses employed (Blank, 1987).

Distinctions must be made between different kinds of day care. Day care provided in a home may be in either a licensed or an unlicensed day care home. (The vast majority of day care homes are not licensed.) Care provided in one's own home may be provided by either a relative or a non-relative. Care provided in a center may take place in either a proprietary or non-proprietary center. Licensing of centers may be required by state or local regulation, but licensing is sometimes evaded. The center may have a high or low adult ratio, and almost an infinite variety of programs exists.

Throughout the years since 1970, controversy has continued over the questions of how much organized child care is needed, what forms such care should take, and what effect day care has on children and their families.

The present study reviews the controversies. Then, taking advantage of what may be termed a "natural experiment"— the subsidizing of day care for low income families in one community—it examines parental views on a variety of forms of day care.

How Much and What Kinds of Organized Child Care?

In 1974, approximately 1.3 million children under age six were in licensed day care or Head Start approved centers (Toward a National Policy for Children and Families, 1976, cited in Bronfenbrenner, Belsky, and Steinberg, 1977), and 4.2 million were enrolled in nursery school and kindergarten (U.S. Bureau of the Census, 1974, cited in Bronfenbrenner, Belsky, and Steinberg, 1977). This makes a total of only 5.5 million places, yet it was estimated that 7.2 million children under age six had parents who worked (Toward a National Policy for Children and Families, 1976, cited in Bronfenbrenner, Belsky, and Steinberg, l977). By 1983, half of the mothers with children under age six were employed, reflecting the need of 9 million children for some form of day care (Thomas, 1986).

A survey conducted by the U.S. Department of Health, Education, and Welfare in 1971 of licensed day care centers and homes also suggested that several million more places for children in day care were needed (Boocock, 1978). Figures cited by Thomas, 1987, *Time,* 1987, and Brydolf, 1987, also suggest a significant need for day care.

The above figures are often cited by day care proponents who contend that these figures can leave no doubt in the public mind that a critical day care shortage does in fact exist.

Other studies suggest that the lack of day care facilities is not the kind of critical issue that is usually suggested by day care proponents. Although some of the data cited is now somewhat dated, it is important to mention it, as it is hailed as significant data by day care opponents. Suzanne Woolsey (1978), in an article entitled "Pied Piper Politics and the Child Care Debate," cites some of these. In both 1965 and 1971, national studies on child care usage were conducted, and in 1973 the Michigan Panel Study of Income Dynamics, also a national survey, included some questions on day care (Low and Spindler, 1968; Jesenius and Shortlidge, 1975; National Consumer Study, 1975).

The 1965 and 1971 surveys indicate similar patterns. The greatest amount of care is in one's home by a relative and the type of care next most utilized is in someone else's home, either by a relative or non-relative. The percentage of families with children under six who utilized care in their own homes increased for both whites and non-whites between 1965 and 1971 (Shortlidge, 1975). The usage of day care centers increased for both whites and non-whites, although the biggest increase was for non-whites (Shortlidge, 1975).

The Westat study of 1970 suggests that for all income groups, the most preferred form of day care by parents of all income groups was care in their own homes or in the neighborhood (Westat, 1970). Proximity to home, cost, hours, program, and availability of sick child care all entered this decision.

The Westat study is often cited to show that more organized child care is not needed. However, the authors specifically conclude, "Findings of the survey indicate there is a sizeable potential demand among low to moderate income working mothers for better day care center capacity. This category of working mothers would like to improve present child care arrangements but would require subsidies to afford better care" (Westat, 1970).

The Shortlidge study also asked questions about preferences for child care. Of the mothers polled, 63 percent (both employed and unemployed) preferred to have their children cared for by relatives over any other arrangement, and 53 percent of the women preferred it to take place in their own homes. Only 24 percent of this sample said that they might select another form of care. [Of this 24 percent, 45 percent would prefer some nursery school or center care (Shortlidge, 1975)].

Some evidence does exist that when high quality day care centers were offered, they were not quickly filled (Westat, 1970). When subsidies were offered in both Denver and Seattle, center care did not increase and the subsidies most often went to informal market care (Kurz, 1975).

Meredith Larson, a staff member at the Stanford Research Institute, after a review of the literature pertaining to day care need, concluded that the need for day care was greatly exaggerated (Larson, 1975). Given the nature of the contradictory findings—the critical need for day care on the one hand and the conclusion that this need is considerably exaggerated on the other hand—a salient question emerged: Are more day care places actually needed, and does this need suggest the desirability of a large national effort?

Two researchers, Sheila Kamerman and Alfred Kahn, suggest that more day care is needed but that the type and extent varies with the age of the child (Kamerman and Kahn, 1979). These researchers contend that a distinctive pattern emerges for children ages three to five. The authors note that 64 percent of three- to five-year-old children are in some type of pre-school program, very often in a packaged form, with nursery school in the morning and day care program in the afternoon.

Kamerman and Kahn assert that since these programs are "private, costly, and beyond the reach for many families, it seems highly unlikely that the demand for such programs has been completely satisfied." They also contend that surveys suggest that most parents want more than just babysitting and seek a program with a strong educational component.

Why are the findings of Kamerman and Kahn so at variance with the conclusions presented by both Larson and Woolsey? Larson based her findings on studies conducted in 1975 and before. One study, Low and Spindler, was done in 1965, and much of the Shortlidge data covers 1967 to 1971. Perhaps as more information has become available to parents emphasizing the importance of early cognitive stimulation, an increasingly large proportion have desired and selected programs which they perceive to have an educational component. It is instructive to note that Kamerman and Kahn specifically cite that the 120 percent increase in nursery school enrollment took place between 1967 and 1976. It is also important to note that more and more mothers are now working; therefore, Kamerman and Kahn would likely find a higher percentage of mothers wanting center care.

The source of information in any study is important. Kamerman and Kahn base their conclusions on the Census, certainly a broader based pool of information than studies based on 50, 100, or even 1,000 interviews.

A study conducted by Karen Hill-Scott in the South Central Los Angeles area also suggests many parents want center care (Hill-Scott, 1978). In Hill-Scott's sample of 779 parents, predominantly black and low income, 47.6 percent preferred center care. Although most studies have found that blacks prefer center care more than whites, this is a much larger percentage than the 1971 Shortlidge study which showed that only fifteen percent of non-whites actually used center care.

Some researchers contend that day care homes are superior to centers. Emlen (1974) is perhaps the strongest proponent for family day care, and delineates its advantages: it accommodates children of any age, requires a minimum of transportation time, and provides a family situation in which parents are able to participate. Emlen cites studies conducted in Portland, Spokane and Pasadena (Emlen, 1974) which found that care givers are usually "nurturant" and "capable."

Other researchers — Peters (1972), Sale (1974), and Prescott (1974) — have found that family day care offers a very child-centered environment. Prescott says that family day care offers a slice of the real world and the opportunity for "horizontal diffusion." By "horizontal diffusion," she means that the family day care mother is often a neighbor or friend, and expresses the same values as the natural mother (Sale, 1973).

Finally, although much of the child care debate may justifiably apply to children in the three-year-old and up category, almost all child care professionals agree that a critical shortage of care for infants (birth to two years old) exists. Because infant care requires a high child–adult ratio, this form of care is the most costly and the most difficult form of care for parents to find.

The question also persists as to whether infants should even be in home or center care, or whether the separation between parent and infant is harmful during the first two years.

In summary, review of the literature offers few guidelines as to how much organized child care is "enough." Judging from the continuing escalation of the employment of mothers of young children and from reports such as Miller's, much more than is presently available will continue to be needed. The literature does show, however, that parental choice is an important factor in determining the forms that day care should take.

Perusal of the literature also raises the interesting question of the influences within the family that shape parental choice.

DAY CARE AND THE FAMILY

While the figures suggest an imminent shortage of day care given the anticipated escalation of working mothers throughout the 1980s and into the 1990s, they fail to tell us about an equally salient issue: What is the relationship between day care and the family?

Only limited research has been conducted on day care and the family. An extensive amount of research has been conducted, however, on day care and its effect on children's cognitive, social, and emotional development (Pardeck, 1986). While this research most often indicates that day care does not have negative effects on children's cognitive abilities and such affective aspects as mother–child attachment, this research must be studied cautiously, for most of it applies only to day care in exemplary settings under the guidance of some of the most knowledgeable people in the early childhood field. We know very little about children in less than exemplary settings.

Another major limitation of this research is its one-sidedness. It examines the impact of day care on children while neglecting to assess the impact of day care on families. Bronfenbrenner suggests that perhaps the most important research is yet to be done:

> Yet, paradoxically, from an ecological perspective, it is the impact of day care beyond the child himself, on the nation's families and the society at large, that may have the more profound consequence for the development of the next generation

of Americans (Bronfenbrenner, Belsky, and Steinberg, 1977, p. 5).

The research on the relationship between day care and the family, although limited, does not indicate family weakening effects. The research has utilized three approaches. The first approach has examined family change over time as a result of the child's enrollment in day care, while the second approach has compared families using day care with home-rearing families as samples. The third approach examines the relationship between length of time in day care and concomitant changes in family life (Bronfenbrenner, Belsky, and Steinberg, 1977).

In an unpublished manuscript, Steinberg and Green (cited in Belsky and Steinberg, 1978) suggested that families utilizing different types of care (babysitters, center, and family day care) reported different changes in their marital relationships (Steinberg and Green, 1978). Parents using babysitters experienced the most positive change in marital relationships, while parents utilizing family day care were least likely to experience a change in family relationships.

Fowler and Khan (1978) compared the effects on early development of children in group care with those in home care. The question, "Is length of stay in early group care associated with any developmental effects?" was posed. The program included a day care program for infants and young children and a parent guidance program which included such topics as cognition, discipline, and play for parents of home-reared children. Parents were visited every two to three months in the child guidance program, and problem families were visited as much as once a week by staff members.

Day care infants were enrolled in waves of twelve each year until there were forty-nine children. Children in both programs were tested on the Griffiths and Binet scales as well as the Bayley Infant Record and the Schaefer and Aaronson Maternal Behavior Inventory.

Fowler reports a consistent but opposite trend for both the home-reared and day care groups. The day care group did better during infancy but declined during the preschool phase of the project, while the home-reared group followed the opposite trend and increased in later development scales, especially in language, fine motor, and practical reasoning. Fowler suggests several possibilities for this finding. When the day care infants reached three years of age, there was a decline in the teacher–child ratio, combined with a higher teacher turnover. Fewer parent visits also took place as the children were older, and parents may have lacked the necessary training to stimulate their preschoolers at as high a level as that which had taken place during infancy. The parents of home-reared infants appeared to become increasingly interested in their children's development, possibly as a concomitant of the repeated testing and the discussion around the testing.

Lally (1977), in the Family Development Research Program, emphasized support for the total family unit and included a program for children aged six to sixty months from high risk environments, as well as a parent program conducted by a child development trainer.

Children were matched with control children on the Cattell Infant Intelligence Scale, the Stanford Binet, and the Early Language Assessment Scale, as well as a variety of Piagetian tasks. Parents were evaluated on the Family Data Record, Home Visit Reports, the Inventory of Home Stimulation, and a staff interview. Few differences were found between groups on the infant tests, but differences were found between program children and controls at thirty-six, forty-eight, and sixty months. When parents were tested on the Stim, which measures the amount of home stimulation given the children, scores were almost identical to the controls at sixty months. However, day care parents did view their children in more positive ways than did the control parents.

Lally states that his program was exploratory in nature and some of the measurement techniques may have been too simplistic. It must also, however, be kept in mind that many of the effects of both Fowler and Lally's programs may show up in future years. Parents who have participated in these programs may become more potent shapers of their children's environments because of the programs' impact.

Another way of assessing the impact of day care on families is by utilizing written questionnaires or personal interviews. Myers, in the Family and Community Day Care Study, assessed the impact of day care on families in Pennsylvania (Myers, 1972). Myers interviewed two groups of parents — one group that had one or more children in day care, while the other group had one or more children on a waiting list. Both urban and rural families were interviewed as well as families using both public and private day care.

Myers concluded that day care mothers had a higher level of marital satisfaction than waiting-list mothers, and employed mothers had a higher level of satisfaction than unemployed mothers. Employed mothers in the day care group had a significantly higher level of marital satisfaction than employed mothers in the waiting-list group.

Golden (1978), in the New York City Day Care Study, attempted to assess the impact of day care on families enrolled in Public Infant Day Care Programs, either center care or family day care (the longitudinal sample), and compared the responses of families with a cross-sectional sample of families whose children entered day care between two-and-a-half and three years of age. Families in the Day Care Program had entered their children between two and twenty-one months and were involved in in-depth interviews both when their children entered the program and when they were thirty-six months old. Families were also assessed on the St. Paul Profile of Family Functioning.

Golden concluded that the families who had been in day care did not differ from the families in the cross-sectional sample who were in the program only a very short time in terms of SES, income from wages, family structure, and total family functioning. However, Golden acknowledges that families may have benefited from programs in ways that were not measured. A study by Catterall (1985) suggests that families using a voucher for day care "upgraded" their lives — paying bills on time and consuming better food with the additional money. Others have argued that day care benefits the child, the family, and, in addition, the total society, with the result that the overall economy runs more smoothly (Zigler, 1982).

The focus of recent research has moved from questioning whether day care is harmful to an understanding of the various types of care already functioning in a community (Siegel and Lawrence, 1984). More recent studies on families have focused on creating a "match" between what the family wants and what is available in the community. A number of studies have dealt with families' use of child care information and referral services (CCI&R).

Besides providing information, some CCI&R agencies have taken on the role of educating parents on what to look for in child care arrangements. An educated parent may have an important impact on services. Educated parents demand better services (Siegel and Lawrence, 1984). However, in many cases people want more information; very often they want a recommendation (Levine, 1982). The problem of recommendations has proven to be so when CCI&R systems have simply provided a list of names. Parents very often want more than a list; they want evaluations.

Researchers such as Levine have noted that although CCI&R fits very nicely into what has been called the Jerry Brown rhetoric that less is more, it is not necessarily the great panacea or the total answer to the child care dilemma. It certainly does not answer the problem of creating more child care places, but only of creating a desirable match between families and presently existing places.

The research conducted thus far on day care and families is scant and offers little solid information. Individuals advocating day care often point to other countries such as Cuba, Russia, Israel, and China and point out the level of quality care that these countries are able to provide for their children. While scrutinizing other countries is indeed important, the diversity of values in American society makes our society quite unique and at variance with most other countries. Perhaps if there is one lesson that we can learn from other countries, it is that child care should support and reinforce families. In our diverse society, not one but many different types of child care are needed.

School Vouchering—An Answer to Family Need?

One possibility for making diverse kinds of child care available to parents is the voucher system. In a voucher system, a family would be allotted a specific amount of money which they could use at the school of their choice. Most of the literature on vouchering pertains to the formal school setting; however, it seems equally relevant for the day care setting where the issues are similar.

The literature pertaining to school vouchering is largely speculative. With the exception of Alum Rock, California (a modified voucher experiment conducted under the auspices of the Office of Economic Opportunity), no real voucher experiment has taken place. The literature on vouchering is primarily concerned with the formal school setting, and is therefore not completely synonymous with the day care situation which is optional and usually encompasses a direct money relationship between the parent and provider. However, day care does offer some of the same dilemmas that the parent would be presented with in the formal school setting under the voucher concept. How does the parent become an informed consumer? How does the parent choose between various alternatives? Does the parent select values entirely similar to the home values or are complementary values sometimes sought? Do parents want homogeneity of social and ethnic groupings, or is heterogeneity valued?

The literature on vouchers encompasses several major areas: the role of parents as consumers, vouchering and its relationship to segregation and integration, the benefit of the poor under a voucher, and the voucher and the consumer analogy, i.e., what control does the individual with a voucher exert over the product? Perhaps the area explored most extensively has been the role of parents in selecting educational settings.

THE ROLE OF PARENTS

Voucher advocates contend that the voucher will permit parents to become informed consumers and potentially make informed choices for their child's education (Coons and Sugarman, 1978; Areen and Jencks, 1972; Coons, 1985; Nathan, 1983). According to Coons and Sugarman, the family will make the best choice for the child's education because the family will bear the ultimate responsibility for that choice.

Whether parents will become informed consumers in selecting schools appears largely a measure of speculation. Some literature pertaining not to the public school setting, but rather to the day care setting (not a vouchered situation), suggests that educated, middle class parents had a very difficult time making intelligent and informed choices in selecting their child's day care (Bradbard and Endsley, 1980). This research makes one wonder whether parents are equipped to select their children's day care or school setting intelligently. If parents are not equipped, what would make them adequately equipped? This remains an open, but important, question.

SEGREGATION OR MEANINGFUL INTEGRATION

Voucher proponents argue that more meaningful racial and social class mixing will be facilitated through the use of vouchers. According to Coons and Sugarman, the integration will be "stable and enduring" (Coons and Sugarman, 1978). Since choice is based less on race and more on educational premises, a more meaningful integration will take place.

Voucher critics argue that people of different social, ethnic, and racial groups do not come together even when it is to their economic advantage (Ginzberg, 1972). New York City is cited as a case in point where whites will forego lower rents in order not to live in the same housing units as blacks (Ginzberg, 1972). Voucher critics contend that less, not more, racial mixing will take place under a voucher (Catterall, 1984).

THE POOR AND THE VOUCHER

Voucher advocates suggest that the poor will benefit under a voucher because they will now have access to many of the school opportunities that were previously available mainly to the rich and the middle class (Coons and Sugarman, 1978; Areen and Jencks, 1971; Coons, 1985; Lewis, 1986). The assumption is that the poor will avail themselves of the many educational options and make informed choices. Poor children will then receive a better education — in many cases an education more responsive to their needs — than the traditional public school education.

However, some literature generates serious questions as to whether the poor will actually receive a better education under a voucher. In a review of the literature on the success of programs for the disadvantaged, Bronfenbrenner suggests that several factors, when they occur together, predict how successful any program will be regardless of its content and methods. Five factors affect program success: employment of the breadwinner, number of children per room in the home, presence of another adult in the home in addition to the caretaker, family income, and the education of the parent (Bronfenbrenner, 1978). When even two or three factors were not present, children were not likely to benefit from any intervention program, while children not subjected to these stressors benefited from whatever program was offered.

Bronfenbrenner's article poses an intriguing question. If the aforementioned factors are directly related to school success, how would the enactment of a voucher program alter more basic institutional patterns, either in the formal school setting or the day care setting?

THE VOUCHER AND THE CONSUMER ANALOGY

It has been suggested by voucher advocates that the consumer can exert his or her influence through voucher dollars and therefore will potentially exert a strong influence on school quality. Schools will be responsive and attentive to consumers in order to generate needed monies (Catterall, 1984).

However, such a direct, simple relationship between consumer and school may not occur. The consumer does not actually own the product and must choose from whatever is offered (Arons, 1971). Schools could "restrict" or "manipulate" what is offered in order to suit their own ends (Arons, 1971). "Hucksters" and false advertising might both operate to entice the unaware consumer (Arons, 1971).

It has also been argued that marketplace analogies simply are not realistic (La Noue, 1971). Research does not exist to show that public schools do better when competition with private schools exists (La Noue, 1971).

Very little literature reports on actual voucher experiments. One very limited voucher experiment took place in Alum

Rock, California, and offered scant information on vouchering.

In Alum Rock, it can certainly be said that the voucher did increase curriculum diversity (teachers did create new programs — bilingual, arts, open-school models), parent interest, and parental satisfaction. However, it cannot be said that parents seized power and helped create massive educational changes. In fact, in the beginning of the experiment parents wanted to maintain the status quo and make sure that they would be guaranteed a place in their neighborhood schools (Cohen and Farrar, 1977). Most parents continued to send their children to neighborhood schools, and most parents did not assume an active or aggressive role in the schools (Cohen and Farrar, 1977). The parent as consumer model held only to a limited extent. Some parents did make curriculum choices and chose different schools, but not many parents. The most active parents were the most educated, and children in voucher schools were from more educated families (Wortman, 1977). Teachers did not compete for students, but this part of the voucher could not really be tested since teachers were guaranteed jobs regardless of how many parents chose them.

The report of the Alum Rock experiment and the available speculative literature provide some information about parental choice as it relates to schooling, but it does not go very deeply into parental values. In the case of day care, what does it mean to parents and what is the interplay between their values and the world of day care?

Parental Choice and Values:
Issues in Understanding Day Care and the Family

The issue of values is critical to the present study. For it is through understanding the concerns, hopes, desires, fears, and aspirations that families hold for their children that we can more fully understand what the day care experience means to the family.

Lillian Rubin, in her introduction to *Worlds of Pain: Life in the Working Class Family* (Rubin, 1976), discusses the importance of studies that delineate the richness of human experience. "Therefore, we need also social science that is so designed;

qualitative studies that can capture the fullness of experience, the richness of living. We need work that takes us inside the dynamics, into the socio-emotional world in which people are born, live, and die; real people with flesh, blood, bones, and skeletons" (Rubin, 1976).

Rubin has captured the hope and pain — the texture of daily life — in the families she interviews. The dreams and the dreamer, love, sex, family, and marriage emerge before us as we more completely understand the complexities and difficulties in the lives of working class families. It is because of Rubin's skill as an interviewer that we understand these families.

The issue of values is directly related to the issue of continuity between home and school settings (Fein, 1973; Powell, 1980). It has been suggested that care in a family day care home might present more continuity for parent and child than care in a center (Fein and Clarke-Stewart, 1973). However, center care, although it represents discontinuity, may be sought because it is a different, more varied form of care than family day care. We need to ascertain how parents perceive the relationship between day care and home. Does day care diminish the authority that parents have over children or is this not a concern?

Another important consideration in any discussion of day care is the meaning, to a parent, of being able to make a choice. Christopher Lasch, for instance, in *Haven for a Heartless World* (Lasch, 1977), argues that the autonomy and privacy of the family have been gradually undermined by giant corporations and mass promotion. Capitalism has appropriated technical knowledge through scientific management and has concomitantly extended control into the workers' private lives through doctors, teachers, and child guidance workers who now supervise child rearing (Lasch, 1977).

Lasch's point is particularly relevant in the context of a significant body of anthropological work which suggests that the needs of the work place determine the form of child rearing. Many teachers, early childhood professionals, and guidance experts have suggested that if lower and working class parents would only change their child-rearing methods, their children would grow up to be more fully functioning individuals and perhaps possess more intellectual ability. However, such experts have usually emphasized the values of flexibility, creativity, and spontaneity—values that are sometimes at odds with the values that working class parents deem important.

It is important to know whether parents feel that they do have a real choice in day care, a choice within which their values are respected. Is the day care available to them meeting the express needs of parents?

Another value issue is the way in which parents perceive the purpose of day care. Day care, as it has done historically, can serve many purposes. It can be viewed as an instrument for achieving the equality of women, an alternative way of raising children, a program that permits people (usually women) to work, or a vehicle for social change. How do parents perceive day care? Do they use it only because they must work or do they also view it as an educational program? How do working parents perceive their many new roles? And how do parents perceive day care as affecting their children? Is it viewed as an enriching experience? Or do some parents feel that they are not as strong an influence on their children—not as strong socializers of their children—because of the influence of day care? Do parents who are from families where the cultural values may suggest that the mother should provide care in the child's early years view day care differently and want different forms of day care than parents without this value system? Regarding the possible effects of child care, or its lack, relatively little systematic study has focused on the interplay between the world of day care and the world of the home.

The Present Study

The existence of subsidized day care in one community offered an opportunity to examine parental choice and values in a context where parents had many choices. The intent of the study was to explore the meaning the day care experience had for families who were supported by subsidies and for other families who were not so supported. Parents were encouraged to speak for themselves on the issues. The study reports what they said.

III

Setting and Methods

In the fall of 1979, this researcher read an article in a day care magazine on the vouchering of day care. The article discussed a subsidized day care program in a northern California community where a subsidy, determined by a sliding scale, was available to parents. Parents were then able to use their subsidy at either a center care program or a family day care program. Parents could choose from programs operated by a community child care group in the city as well as private programs which were certified by the community child care program. The author realized that a study of this system could reveal much about parent choice and parent values.

This study took place in a community which includes a university. The university helps create a cosmopolitan feeling to this community of approximately 56,000 people. Although many professionals live in the community, the poor, though not as obvious, are also present. They live in cramped apartments, subsidized housing, or small houses.

To what extent the findings of the present inquiry reflect the unique characteristics of this community is uncertain. The study of parental choice in larger cities that have experimented with subsidies, such as Oakland, California, and Boston, Massachusetts, or in a statewide system such as Florida, might yield different results.

Community Child Care

The Community Child Care (CCC) is an autonomous board composed of parent users and interested community

23

members. It is funded by the city and county and parent fees. The CCC operates ten day care centers which meet stringent guidelines more exacting than state and federal regulations. The centers include infant care, preschool programs, and after school care. Each program includes places for both full paying families and subsidized families.

In addition, private day care programs and family day care homes can join the subsidized program by meeting the standards of the CCC Standards Committee. A CCC evaluation team assesses each interested program on a variety of indices and makes a written report, including the areas of child development, quality of staff, sound nutrition, adequate salaries, and adequate equipment. Private programs include day care homes and an infant center.

Because of the quality controlled programs in this city — both private programs and CCC programs — a wide variety of options are available for parents. The parent looking for day care is expected to make choices. Contends one CCC coordinator, "It's expected that the parent will go visiting and choose the center best suited to her and the child's needs" (Majteles, 1979). Because the Community Child Care pays the difference between what the family can pay, as determined by a sliding scale fee, and what the provider charges, parents have a very real choice and not a limited choice based simply on what they can afford. Every parent pays at least a minimum of $.20 per hour. The maximum amount paid by a subsidized parent is $.20 below the program's per hour charge. When this researcher was conducting the study, the hourly rate for preschool programs was $1.39.

THE SITES

Each program in the CCC has a unique tone. Parents in this study are represented from the following programs:

Cambridge: Open from 7:00 A.M. to 6:00 P.M. and serving twenty-four children, two-and-a-half years to kindergarten age. Cambridge is very close to the university but is located in a residential neighborhood. It has a large open inside area and a sloping green lawn. Cambridge is known as the program that has a cognitive developmental philosophy and emphasizes learning through play.

Muir: Muir accommodates twenty-four children in the two to five age range, and is open from 8:00 A.M. to 2:30 P.M. It is in a very crowded downtown area. It has three small rooms and a yard wedged between several streets. Muir is known as a program that emphasizes self reliance through independence.

Maybeck: Maybeck accommodates thirty children, ages two-and-a-half to five years. It is one block from one of the busiest streets in the city and is housed in a former school. The yard has several climbing structures and much grass. This program is known as the center that emphasizes socialization skills.

Sierra: Sierra is open from 7:30 A.M. to 6:00 P.M. and accommodates twenty-four children, two years six months to kindergarten. It is housed in part of a church, off a busy street. Sierra has an extensively developed inside environment that seems to blend with the beautiful surrounding outside area. Sierra is known as a child-centered play environment that emphasizes social, emotional skills.

Clayton: Clayton accommodates thirty children in the kindergarten age group. Clayton is in a former public school and is open from 12:00 noon to 6:00 P.M. It emphasizes many creative afternoon choices.

Phoenix: Phoenix accommodates twelve infants, two months to three years of age. Its hours are 7:30 A.M. to 5:30 P.M. Phoenix is located behind a church in three small rooms, with a small grassy yard. Phoenix bases its program on a specific developmental theory that emphasizes

the "whole child." It is also known for its
individualized, caring approach.

Hawthorne: Hawthorne accommodates thirty infants, ages
two months to three years. It is open from 7:00
A.M. to 6:00 P.M. Hawthorne is housed in a
former school and utilizes two classrooms — one
for infants and one for toddlers.

Carter: Carter accommodates twelve children, ages two
months to two years, from 7:30 A.M. to 5:30
P.M. It is housed in a small two-story house and
uses the downstairs for school and the upstairs
for offices. Carter has a flat yard with both
sand and grass.

Rosewood: Rosewood accommodates twenty children, ages
four months to three years, and is open from
7:00 A.M. to 5:30 P.M. Rosewood is off a busy
street, but is in a residential area. It is located
in the wing of a church. Rosewood has three
small rooms and a huge, spacious yard. It
bases its program on the same theorist as
Phoenix.

Each center, except the kindergarten program, has a parent
education component. The infant–toddler centers have
monthly meetings and the preschool programs have meetings
every few months. All centers, whether they have infants,
toddlers, or preschoolers, have individual conferences with
parents at least twice a year. The after school programs have
conferences once a year. All centers have a bulletin board with
a variety of items listed, including such things as menus and
parent education information.

Most of the staff have at least BA degrees. In addition,
many staff hold MA degrees.

There is a very low staff turnover in most programs. This
low turnover appears to be for several reasons. First, the pay
is good in comparison to many other child care situations.
Secondly, there appears to be much emphasis on both staff
meetings and staff decision making. Staff issues are treated

seriously. For instance, the CCC organization is currently working on ways to reward longevity of service.

DAY CARE HOMES

Three day care homes were visited in this study.

Mrs. R's: Mrs. R's Day Care Home is located in a modern, spacious house off a busy street. Mrs. R has six preschool and toddler children. She provides art activities in the morning and offers free choice activities in the afternoon.

Mrs. M's: Mrs. M's Day Care is located in a small home in a residential neighborhood. Mrs. M has children from infancy through preschool. She offers a variety of activities inside and outside her program. Her home is quite small, as is her yard. She believes in close communication with parents.

Mrs. J's: Mrs. J has preschoolers. Her day care home is located off a lovely residential street. She has a large family room that opens onto a beautiful yard. She offers many inside and outside activities and also takes the children on numerous trips.

Parents making a choice can choose from this variety of programs. They can choose from different physical environments (inside and out), staff, location, hours, philosophies, and ethnic composition. The ethnic composition varies from program to program and year to year, depending on which particular families choose which particular programs.

Assessment of Centers

To have some context for interpreting the comments made by the parents, the researcher visited each center a minimum of two times. Each home was visited once. Centers were all assessed on the Bradbard and Endsley Teaching Guide (Bradbard and Endsley, 1980). This guide includes:

(1) Health and Safety—Floors are carpeted or have a nonskid covering. The physical environment is safe, with no jagged edges or other physical health hazards.

(2) Adult–Child–Peer Interaction—Enough adults are available so that children can be given individual attention if needed. Adults are warm; they hug, smile, cuddle, and speak appropriately to children.

(3) Home–Center Coordination—Lunch and snack menus are posted. When parents arrive and leave, there is a discussion about the child's day at school or information shared about the child at home.

(4) Physical Characteristics of the Center—The outdoor area has both soft and hard surfaces. A variety of large muscle activities can take place in the outside area.

(5) Materials and Equipment—Attractive books and toys are available for children. Toys are safe, with no jagged edges, loose buttons, or wires.

The Bradbard and Endsley Teaching Guide has been used in other studies of child care settings. It enabled the researcher to compare the centers on specific criteria as well as to get the "feeling" or "tone" of each.

THE SELECTION OF FAMILIES

Fifty parents were interviewed for this study; thirty-five families received a subsidy. Four families had lost the subsidy because their income had gone up or because they had moved but were asked to answer the questions from the point of view of being on the subsidy. Of the fifty parents interviewed, forty-six were women and four were men.

Subsidy amounts varied, depending on the family's income and the number of children in the family.

Families were represented in a number of occupations. Non-subsidized families were usually professionals—lawyers, accountants, and computer analysts being represented in this category. Subsidized families were represented in a number of categories — "pink collar" jobs — women in offices making a very limited wage, assembly workers, the self-employed, part-time workers, and students.

Families were selected in various ways. Some directors asked this researcher to give them a letter explaining the research. Such directors then asked parents if they wished to participate in the study. They then gave names and telephone numbers of those who agreed to be involved in the research. At other centers this researcher greeted parents personally at the door, explained the research project to them, and asked if they were willing to participate. Most parents were very interested in the study and said they would like to be interviewed.

The Interviews

This researcher, when designing the study, weighed the pros and cons of various research possibilities such as the questionnaire or structured interview. The open-ended semi-structured interview was selected because of its potential for getting in-depth information and for probing for additional information. The interview format provided some structure and at the same time offered an opportunity for parents to talk freely about many areas of child care as well as how they were socialized as children and how this influenced their parenting practices (see Interview Schedule, Appendix A).

Parents were free to select the place where they would be most comfortable during the interview. Many parents were interviewed at their homes or apartments. Others were interviewed at their child's playground or over coffee at a local coffee house. Parents seemed genuinely pleased to have an opportunity to talk about their children, child care, and hopes and dreams for the future.

Interviews were tape recorded so that the researcher could maintain good eye contact and, at the same time, get information exactly the way it was stated by parents. Tape recordings proved invaluable in assessing the meaning of parental statements.

Interviews ranged from twenty-five minutes to an hour. Some people spoke briefly, while others had a great deal to say about each topic. Few parents seemed reluctant to be taped, and there is no indication that those who were spoke more briefly.

Parents were explicitly told that this researcher was not part of the Child Care system. The skills of an interviewer contribute greatly to the adequacy of the material obtained in an interview. If the interviewees are to feel free to express both negative and positive feelings, the interviewer needs to guard against shaping their responses by his or her comments, facial expressions, or gestures.

The interview schedule was designed to encourage the expression of different points of view. For example, some questions were worded, "Some people feel this way and other people feel that way. How do you feel?"

As the interviewer, the researcher drew on earlier experience that she had had with similar interview schedules. She saw herself as a good listener and one who was unlikely to register surprise, shock, or disapproval at any answer. She was aware that, as a professionally educated teacher with several years of experience in preschool and elementary school, she brought to the study her own set of preferences and values. She resolved to hold these in abeyance as she listened to what the parents said and as she considered its meaning.

INTERVIEWS WITH DIRECTORS

Day care center and home directors were also interviewed using a semi-structured open-ended interview. This interview format allowed directors to speak freely about their programs and, at the same time, focused the discussion. Interviewing directors provided still another perspective on day care in this northern California community (see Interview Schedule, Appendix B).

Analysis of the Data

All tapes were coded with identifying numbers. Pertinent data were then transcribed by hand.

The researcher noted the points made by each respondent to questions related to a particular issue or theme. These points were then listed so that for any single question the researcher was able to look at the responses of all fifty parents. For direct quotations, illustrating different kinds of responses, the researcher went back to the original tapes.

Anonymity

To assure anonymity for participants in the study, certain identifying features have been altered throughout the report.

In Chapters III through VIII, the parents present their views. The directors have their opportunity in Chapter IX.

Changed Roles — New Roles

My mother was a real mother. . . . She was home baking cookies, doing the mother things.

(Stated by a busy young accountant
with one child and another on the way)

Daniel Yankelovich, in *New Roles: Searching for Self Fulfillment in a World Turned Upside Down,* discusses the changed attitudes Americans express on a variety of subjects, including families (Yankelovich, 1981). One is struck in the present study by the changed roles that have taken place in one generation. Almost all the parents in this study were raised in two-parent families with mothers who were either homemakers or entered the work force when their children were in the school-age or high school years. Whether respondents were raised in professional or blue collar families, their perceptions of their mothers' roles were amazingly similar.

A young, divorced mother comments: "My mother was home all the time," and a single parent raising a son states, "There were six of us and my father worked. My mom stayed home and took care of us." Yet these very parents have put their children into day care, many when the children were as young as three months.

It is particularly interesting to note that many parents, when they were growing up, did not see themselves becoming working parents. One young mother who works in a hospital business office comments:

I thought of myself as being home. I never thought I'd like to put

32

my child in day care. It seemed like an alienating sort of experience.

A married mother with two young children states:

My mother stayed at home until I was in high school. . . . I grew up thinking that's the way I was going to be.

Many other parents in the study expressed similar thoughts. Yet with these varied thoughts as children and adolescents, all these parents are now either working or students. How can one explain such a phenomenon? Parents who were not sure at all what they were going to be now are either in the work force or student force. Certainly, the current economic situation could offer a possible reason for this phenomenon. Most parents who work today must work. The 1970s brought an increase in single-parent families and escalating inflation (Ruopp and Travers, 1982). However, a far more cogent reason is offered by Yankelovich (1981). Yankelovich proposes the concept of the "Giant Plates of Culture." He presents an "image of the earth moving deep beneath the surface and so transforming the landscape that it loses its comfortable familiarity . . . the 'giant plates' of American culture shifting relentlessly beneath us. The shifts create huge dislocations in our lives. Those living closest to society's fault lines are the first to be thrown into new predicaments. But even those living at a remote distance feel the tremor" (Yankelovich, 1981).

It appears that these parents have been affected by the "Giant Plates of Culture." Perhaps one of the most startling changes in Americans is the changing perception of both self-fulfillment and independence as important goals for both men and women. Housewife is no longer a satisfactory choice, nor is it likely to be for the children of the respondents in this study. As Yankelovich states, "The Plates of Culture do not shift backwards" (Yankelovich, 1981).

Much research is linear, investigating the affects of parents upon child. But what about the effects of the present generation upon their own parents? Has this generation, whose values have altered, had an effect on their own parents? Many of the parents in this study report discovering, some with amazement, that their own parents either approve or do not have negative feelings about their grandchildren being in day care. In fact, only five of the parents report that their own parents express negative feelings about their grandchildren being in day care. Many respondents perceive that their own lives are much more interesting and rewarding than the housewife role their mothers had assumed. Some mothers recognize that their own ambitions and diverse roles have made their mothers examine their own lives. (For fathers in this study, their own parents assumed that they would aspire to careers.)

One mother with two young children, a preschooler and a toddler, comments:

> They [my parents] think it's wonderful. I think a lot of the older generation feels that maybe the women missed out because they didn't have the opportunity to work . . . and they couldn't pursue work.

A young computer analyst with one toddler, states:

> I really enjoy the time I'm with Janice and I really enjoy the time I'm at work. And I think my mother saw that the last time she visited. . . . I almost felt a feeling of envy in that my mother, who never had a career, felt that this was really a better way to go at it and that made me feel kind of good.

Other parents report that although their own parents were initially concerned about their grandchildren in child care, once they began to observe the progress of their grandchildren or the specific programs, they appeared to overcome these concerns. A married mother of three who runs her own small business comments:

> Initially, my mom sort of balked at everything I did. . . . She went and visited the children's center and she could see Sam was doing well. . . . She thought it was a very stimulating environment and would be helpful for him. She was supportive after a while, but initially she was sort of skeptical.

A married mother with one toddler, who teaches emotionally disturbed children, notes:

> She [mom] is pretty accepting and I think she's been more accepting because she's seen how he's grown and what a

really happy and secure child he is. And I think for her that has been really important.

A married mother with two young girls comments:

They [my parents] always hoped that I would somehow find a way to stay out of work. . . . When that didn't happen, they were reassured about the kind of care they [the girls] are getting and now are just totally over any feelings they had.

A mother separated from her husband, with two small girls — one in infant care and one in preschool — comments:

My mom thinks it's great because she learns so many things there [at day care]. She is able to learn social aspects, living with other people, too.

For many of the grandparents the "proof is in the pudding." They have seen how independent many of their grandchildren are and how they appear to be thriving in the day care situation. It is also likely that these grandparents themselves have been influenced by the plethora of articles, newspaper accounts, and television shows which suggest that children can learn a great deal at young ages and that professionals have a great deal to teach children.

It must be mentioned that not all grandparents are delighted with a day care program. Three grandparents express disapproval, while one says that she wishes her daughter had stayed home, and another feels "funny" about a day care program. And one respondent states, "My mother wished I had asked her to help."

The changes in perceptions of women's roles are significant whether parents in this study were raised in blue collar working-class families or upper-income professional families, whether they were raised in the suburbs or the city. The term *homemaker* is simply not in their vocabularies. It is not that they do not want to ensure that their children are nurtured — they do. It is rather that staying home to ensure secure, nurtured children (the roles with which most of them grew up) does not seem at all feasible nor desirable, and in the words of one parent, "I think it's just crazy that women have to have a family or a job. We have to have the two options — the two possibilities at the same time."

IV

Many Parents — Many Choices

The most important thing was that I have a rapport with the staff; that I liked the people. . . . This particular center stood out in my mind because of the staff.

> (Stated by a young professional mother with one
> child, who had looked at numerous programs
> before deciding on her child's placement)

The Community Child Care (CCC) system encourages parents to look at several day care programs, and forty of the parents in this study did visit more than one program. Only three of the respondents looked at only one day care program. Many respondents make an arduous search before they place their children in a center or family day care home. This is true whether parents are or are not subsidized. A young mother with a toddler, whose boyfriend had died in a boat accident before their son was born, comments:

> I looked at Rosewood and Hawthorne and two day care homes, one of which I felt so-so about . . . and the one had animals around. And then I looked at Hawthorne and was pretty happy with that . . . and I've been very happy.

And a married mother with two young children, one in infant care and one in a preschool program, who had lost her subsidy after her income went up, comments:

> We [my husband and I] took a lot of time off work together. We went to lots of centers and observed a couple of hours and

went back again so we could see what kind of facilities they had. . . . And when we walked in to Maybeck, we felt such warmth . . . and we liked the non-sexist, non-racist part of it.

A low-income parent who has never married and has two young children, notes:

I visited Maybeck, Cambridge, Sierra, and I was also looking for something that was not too structured in its approach.

Sometimes the experience of visiting a center generates ideas on what should be included in other programs. One parent notes:

I went to Muir and everything looked just fine. After that I looked at other programs to see if they had some of the same elements as the Muir Center.

Parents have definite feelings as to why they selected the particular program. Many times they go by a "feeling," a "tone," and overwhelmingly, they select a program where the staff feels "warm." The selection of a program because of the warmth and "caring staff" emerges in thirty-four of the responses. A young professional mother comments, "When you walked in to Maybeck . . . you just felt such warmth."

A recently divorced mother, struggling to care for her four-year-old child, notes:

The center that I'm at now—I've been very spoiled because it's uncommonly warm and family-like. The thing that impressed me most was the sense of caring by the staff.

A young father comments that he would not compromise on

. . . the good teachers who have a real sense of caring and fondness for that age group. And I guess a real sense of responsibility on their part in the fact that they have a very valuable part of my life in their care all day long.

Several parents mentioned that convenience of location is important in a day care setting, several parents mentioned space, and several parents mentioned the hours the center is open. Clearly, it is the quality of the staff that is the single major criterion for most parents. This is true whether parents are considering a program in the downtown area, which is literally wedged between several city streets, or whether they are considering a spacious program located in a residential neighborhood.

However, it must be noted that this city is a geographically small area with an excellent transportation system. Choosing one center or program over another, in many cases, means only a few minutes difference in driving time.

When parents were asked to mention their gut level response on one or two important things which they could not compromise in any day care program, the topic of staff came up in twenty-five of the responses. A scientist with one preschool child states:

> You've got to have good people who know what they're doing. . . . You can really damage a little kid . . . so it's the people first. You have to have good people.

A single mother, struggling to make ends meet, commented on how she felt when she went to the new infant center, "I just knew . . . the people; it was just great."

For some parents the day care has become an extended family, and for these parents staff is critical. One mother, raising her preschool child alone, with her parents away in Maine, comments:

> The staff at our center are just so warm and caring that I really do feel a sense of extended family.

Another parent, who came from another country, discusses her fondness for the director at her child's school:

> She [Margaret] is a friend with the adults, which is important, especially since we don't have family here.

The second item mentioned by parents as important in a day care program is health and safety. However, this is mentioned by only seven parents. The fact that health and safety are mentioned by such a paucity of parents is probably due to the fact that many parents express great confidence in the

CCC system of assessing programs. They therefore may take health and safety for granted. Proximity is mentioned by five parents, staff ratio by three, and a lack of rigidity by two parents.

It is not that parents do not want many specific activities — they do. It is simply that warmth and the quality of staff are considered the overriding, salient issues. Perhaps this is not surprising. When parents are not present for a large part of the day, the parent may well perceive that it is his or her warmth and love which are not present, and it is therefore imperative that these be provided by the adults in charge. Parents perceive that the qualities of warmth and love are critical to healthy child development.

It is interesting to note that the debates on curriculum that are prominent in the minds of most professionals and are given significant consideration in child care journals and educational magazines are not uppermost in the minds of these parents. Most parents will not put their children in a physically lovely facility, even if they perceive the activities are excellent, if they do not perceive the child care teachers as caring individuals. Many of these parents seem to be saying that they must feel some bond with the child care teacher before they themselves can leave their children with confidence. Perhaps they are also saying, after they feel a bond with staff, their child will also feel a bond with staff.

It is possible that one of the most salient factors from the child's point of view is the match between what the parent considers as caring staff and what the parent perceives as warmth from the child's point of view. If indeed parents are able to find a level of warmth compatible with their own, it would suggest a significant intersection between home and school in the emotional domain.

ACTIVITIES

Parents do want many activities in the program and they perceive many activities as taking place. Parents, in a sense, "want it all."

Parents, overwhelmingly, want what educators might call a "traditional" program. The term "traditional" is being used to describe a program which has a basic time structure, e.g., morning activities, lunch, and afternoon activities, but within that structure offers rich and varied choices. However, it must be mentioned that while programs have a traditional tone to them, they also have their own particular philosophies which permeate the programs — the program which addresses independent learning, the program based on the philosophy that socialization skills are primary, etc. Thirty-five of the parents discussed this traditional program — a program with art, cooking, and inside and outside activities. A mother of a four-year-old child notes:

> What was important for him [Sam] was to be able to communicate. . . . It [the center] could help me in some of those difficult areas so he could learn to get along with other children. . . . And I was also looking for something where every day he could go and look forward to a new activity, so that his life was just as rich as mine . . . and to have a fun experience at an early age.

A student with a preschool child comments:

> One thing that I am very happy about is the center itself. I feel that the children there have free time. I mean, they have lots of art prepared for them but they are free to do whatever they want or not to do any one of the projects they have set up for them. . . . I like the arts . . . all the choices that improve creativity and social and emotional skills.

A mother of six children who has recently separated from her husband remarks:

> I don't want my children in a structured learning program that has certain goals for certain ages. . . . I want [activities] . . . a huge variety of activities, art and puzzles, and big stuff outdoors, and a lot available in terms of stimulation.

The fact that parents want a traditional program has several explanations. It could be that parents, whether they had or had not been exposed to the CCC system, would have wanted traditional programs. However, it is also possible that because CCC offers a variety of traditional programs, the very exposure to traditional programs has in turn shaped parental ideas.

It is also very possible that these programs bring satisfaction precisely because they also bring choice. They bring a choice of programs, philosophy, a choice of such factors as hours, physical characteristics, and teacher personality. The parent can therefore match his or her own philosophy with the particular philosophy and tone of the day care program, thus creating a harmonious interface between home and the day care situation.

Many parents perceive the world of day care as much richer and offering many more options than the home situation. The world of day care is a child-centered world. The world of home is a place where adults and children must share space and therefore offers more restrictions. The world of home has real parents with their own needs to be taken into account, whereas the world of day care has many activities planned just for children. It is a child's place, a child's world.

A mother of a preschooler who owns her own business notes:

> Day care has a variety of things to do, and that's the thing that day care can provide more than I can do because they have such a terrific play yard—with a sand area and swings and the water, and I can't do a whole lot of that. . . . They also have a whole lot of books and toys and it's just impossible to do that for one child when they can do it for twenty.

And another parent, a writer, with a toddler and a preschooler comments:

> I like him to be in that environment where there are things for them to do and everything is for them. . . . You know there's things here that are not allowed because adults live in the house as well as children, so in that environment it's for the kids and there's not many things that are out of bounds that they're not allowed to do.

DISCIPLINE

When parents are asked about the type of discipline that is important and if the discipline is similar to or different from the discipline in day care, thirty-three of the parents find the discipline at the center similar to their own form of discipline.

A single parent raising one preschool child, comments:

> I liked what they did there [the center] in that they had the children—if two children were in disagreement about something and there was a fight starting or something, they would have them talk to the children and try to find out what's going on and they would have the children talk to each other and have a dialogue and come to some kind of resolution . . . and that's similar to what I do at home.

A young student with a preschooler notes:

> I think [discipline] is pretty much the same. . . . In Maybeck they try to make the child very responsible and self-disciplined, and we try here at home to do the same thing.

However, a prevailing theme emerges when parents discuss discipline. They know they should be good disciplinarians but many times they feel that they do not have the skills. A single mother comments:

> My sense of discipline—uh, that's actually kind of hard for me. That's the one point where I feel the least strong about being a single parent. I don't like that I have to be always the person to discipline and those are the times when I wish for other voices and other hands to help assess the situation.

A graduate student working on a doctorate in economics says:

> I feel that in terms of discipline I'm very confused. I, to regress a little bit, was pretty much raised as an only child and I'd never baby-sat. I was the kind of person who was never involved with children so I don't know anything about kids . . . and I've never even taken child psychology . . . and I probably vacillate about discipline.

Similarly, a mother with one preschool child comments:

> I'm a very bad discipliner . . . and it's hard for me to get the child to do what I want her to do. . . . It's even difficult for me to speak loud.

Interestingly enough, it is the child care center that offers support, acts as a sounding board, and serves as a model for discipline. Seventeen of the parents in the study spontaneously discussed the ways in which the child care program helps them deal with discipline. These comments were completely spontaneous since this researcher did not ask if the day care program helped with discipline.

Child care staff acts as a model. The father of two young girls, a preschooler and a toddler, states:

> I think they [the center] have a very constructive approach, which is that they encourage the kids as they become verbal to use words to explain what they're feeling and to explain what they want out of a situation rather than non-verbal stuff. . . . A lot of that kind of grew into an attitude we have about kids and discipline as we got involved with the center and saw how effectively that can work. . . . We've learned some attitudes about our own parenting from the center.

A mother, recently separated from her husband, notes:

> When Jackie first started here, I would say, "You are bad for doing this." Well, they had kind of switched it to, "You are doing a bad thing," so I kind of took that on also.

A mother with two preschool children, comments:

> I think I've learned a lot from the way they are doing their discipline. I feel I've learned to be more gentle and understanding than I would be if I hadn't watched. . . . Because I watch the teachers and I really admire the way they're disciplining the children and they don't discipline them so much, but they treat them with a lot of respect.

The center also helps with specific behavior problems. One mother comments on a typical two-year-old behavior problem—biting:

> There was a problem with biting . . . and the more I thought about their [the center's] approach, the better it sounded. . . . Their approach really was to try to minimize the whole incident if you're talking about a sporadic incident, which it was, . . . especially as a first-time mother first encountering the problem; that's the opposite of the reaction you're going to have.

However, for some parents the discipline in the day care

program is not similar to the discipline at home. Several parents find that at the center there is much more clarity about discipline than exists in the home. Several parents also state that there is more talking at the center. At home, when they are short-tempered, they give the child a smack. They state that smacking, or any form of corporal punishment, would never be tolerated at the center.

Disciplinary situations provide a fine context in which to observe the interface of professional and parent. This researcher had the opportunity to observe discipline in the various centers and in two homes, and indeed the perception of parents is most accurate. Staff does model excellent behavior, adult voices are low and controlled, and misbehavior is redirected. Not once did this researcher hear a child ridiculed or scolded. Avoiding this is surely an impossible task for most parents. Most early childhood educators would agree that discipline and the development of inner controls is a critical area of child development.

It is not at all surprising that parents are unsure about discipline. Not only do most parents not have an extended family to offer advice and guidance, but parents are inundated with a variety of books and articles on discipline. Many of these books offer contradictory advice. For example, where Ginott (1969) offers reasoning and respect, Bodenhamer (1983) suggests that the role of reasoning is exaggerated and in many cases parents should simply tell their children what is expected and follow through. Some professionals advise parents to use behavior modification techniques for even minor problems, whereas other professionals scorn these techniques. No wonder parents are confused!

In the area of discipline, it appears that the professional often guides and the parent learns. Although there are many times when parents and staff collaborate on children's problems, it appears that often it is the professional who sets clear standards and offers positive models. Most parents are only too glad to have the opportunity to observe and learn.

While many children are in day care centers, family day care homes are also an option. What perceptions do families using them have?

FAMILY DAY CARE

The theme of center care versus family day care is one of the most emotionally charged topics for parents in this study. It is true that most of the parents interviewed had chosen center care, but parents initially had the choice between center care and family day care. This researcher tried very hard to find more subsidized families in family day care. However, since relatively few families were in family day care subsidized places, it was most difficult to locate any.

In the day care literature, researchers Emlen (1974) and Sales (1973) have argued strongly for family day care, noting its ability to offer a "slice of the real world" and the possibilities for horizontal diffusion between care giver and parent. Emlen has also noted its convenience, low cost, and ability to offer care for several children in the same family.

The parents in this study do not share the enthusiasm for family day care offered by Sales (1973) and Emlen (1974). In fact, only three of the parents prefer family day care, and an additional four of the parents state that family day care might be better for infants and young children. One parent says she does not really have a preference; either situation is fine.

Why then do so many parents prefer center care? Many parents have been very impressed by the media accounts of family day care where gross injustices have been reported, such as the Nathan case where a child actually died. Accounts of bizarre happenings at day care centers had not occurred at the time of the study. A mother of two young boys, one a preschooler and one a toddler, comments:

> I think there's a risk when you go into a day care home situation. It was before the publicity about what's her name? . . . Lori, what's her name?—but even so, you heard horror stories of various things that happened.

A young professional mother comments that when her toddler was an infant:

> I never felt comfortable with putting him in someone else's home. I would not know what was happening in someone else's home. . . . I guess I was afraid of abuse and even not so

much physical abuse as just the way he would be treated. I would never know in someone else's home.

As parents discussed their preference for center care, they linked this discussion with what they do not like about family day care. Parents worry because there is only one caretaker. How can they really be certain that the person is trustworthy? In a center, several adults are present. One mother, working in a hotel and who has a disabled husband, comments:

> In the center you have lots of people in there—lots of families in there, and if something were to go wrong and if I did not catch it, another family would see it.

Since the center offers several adults, if a child does not get along with one caretaker, there is always another caretaker that the child can relate to. A mother with one preschool child comments:

> He'd be around different adults . . . and if there was one he didn't like, there'd be another one he did like. There was always, at any given time, someone he did like.

A center also offers standards that can be enforced and maintained. Comments one mother of an infant:

> I feel I'm very pro center environment because I feel that the parent has more control because they're adhering to standards. They've got a staff with a minimal amount of training versus if you're dependent on one mother who may or may not be sick, whose standards may vary like anyone else's from day to day. I just don't feel that parent has as much control over one individual as they have over an institution.

Another parent with an infant posits:

> This is open to the public. . . . There are people in and out all the time. People are never alone with the children. There is always more than one adult.

Many parents believe that a home cannot offer the same quality program that is offered in a center. Parents often perceive a home as offering babysitting and a center as offering a quality program. A young mother of a preschooler, recently a student and now pregnant with her second child, who had chosen a center, comments:

> Family day care doesn't have the right tools, or right toys, or right materials for the kids to play with. . . . It was very important for a nice outside place and a good place inside.

Another mother who is currently a student and who has a preschooler notes:

> I think the activities in the center care are much more organized and structured towards the age of the children and towards their rate of comprehension. . . . Also there is more space and there are more toys, a variety of toys, and a variety of people to relate with.

Another common fear is that if a parent's child is in family day care, and the day care mother's own child is sick, or there is an emergency in the day care mother's family, the day care mother might well cancel day care. This actually happened to several parents in the study, although these family day care programs were not part of CCC.

Six of the parents in this study did use family day care at one point, but several of these parents were not satisfied with the care and subsequently chose center care. One young mother, divorced and with two children under four years of age in a family day care home under the CCC subsidy program, was hoping that she would be able eventually to get both of her children into a center where she perceived a richer program.

Although parents have very vivid ideas and images about home care, very few parents have actually visited child care homes. The reasons for not wanting homes are therefore based on word of mouth, individual preference, and the stereotypes home care has received largely through newspaper and television coverage.

Most parents consider center care as warm and more caring than family day care. In the words of one mother:

> . . . He goes to a center which you might consider an institu-

tion. . . . I don't feel he's institutionalized . . . because of the warmth.

Perhaps it is a combination of factors that makes center care such a positive alternative in this study. It is not only the fact that family day care has received much adverse press coverage, but also the fact that parents want what they perceive to be a "real" program. Parents perceive this real program to include a strong curriculum, facilitated by a highly trained staff.

The Role of CCC in Choice Making

Parents make choices, but how do they know where to begin? Child care literature has suggested that an important component in choosing child care is the role of the referral agency. Research in this study confirms this. Thirty of the parents in the study used the services of CCC. Often this involves simply getting a list of names and addresses of various programs from CCC. In many cases parents felt great confidence in simply receiving a CCC approved list because they had heard that CCC set very high standards in both the CCC run centers and the CCC approved subsidy programs. One mother commented, and she spoke for many other parents, "Since it was CCC, I didn't have any problem with it. . . . All the centers have good staffs."

Parents perceive CCC as offering information but wanting parents to make the final choice. Noted one mother, "CCC is helpful. . . . The people working there are very good at giving out information and helping parents make their decisions and leaving the decision up to the parents as much as possible."

The feeling of confidence in the CCC organization cannot be overestimated. Bradbard and Endsley in an article entitled "Helping Parents Become Day Care Consumers" (Bradbard and Endsley, 1980) suggest that many parents do not know where to begin when they look for day care. As one mother in Bradbard and Endsley's study noted, and she spoke for many other mothers, she "let her fingers do the walking" (Bradbard and Endsley, 1980). Obviously, every program tries to make itself sound attractive, which leaves parents with very few guidelines when selecting day care. Because parents feel that CCC sets high standards and the parent is therefore not likely to make a great mistake when selecting a CCC program or a CCC approved subsidized program, they seem to venture forth in their search for day care with much greater confidence.

In conclusion, parents do look at different day care programs. Although some parents may ultimately choose a program because it is nearer to their work location or because the hours, full- or part-time, are what they need or because they are next on the waiting list for a particular program, most parents interviewed make a conscientious, deliberate choice. Parents seem very clear in describing what they want. Most parents interviewed want a rich and varied program with many options for their children and they want this program taught by a well-trained staff. However, choosing staff involves many choices since particular personalities are more or less appealing based on the particular personality of the parent. Choosing programs also involves another level of choice since various programs have specific foci and philosophies. Most parents want and appreciate the help they get from the center around the issue of discipline, an area about which they express much concern. These parents want choices and seem appreciative of the many choices which they indeed do have.

V

Day Care and Home—
A World of Continuity or Discontinuity?

Without realizing it, we tend to point out or emphasize some cognitive aspect of things. And one of the things we actively looked for were programs that were not heavily cognitive oriented. We were looking for a balance. I think we probably looked to all the child care situations as a way to expand on or enhance rather than substitute for what we were doing at home.

(Stated by a father with two young girls)

While it is true that parents are able to make choices and select programs, the salient question still emerges—Does day care offer a world of continuity or discontinuity between the home/school setting? This is a topic that has been raised by a number of educators and researchers (Powell, 1980; Fein and Clarke-Stewart, 1977).

The interface and intersection between home and day care is a topic about which we know relatively little. For instance, while continuity may be perceived as a positive quality, it is also possible that discontinuity between home and day care, in some cases, might also be perceived as positive.

Two themes suggesting the possibility of continuity and/or discontinuity have been previously delineated. One is the theme of activities and the other the theme of discipline. Parents perceive the activities at day care as richer and more varied than they can provide at home. However, parents do not experience this difference in program as an experience of discontinuity, but simply as additional stimulation for the child. Parents offer additional experiences to their children all the time. When they sign their children up for swimming lessons or a science class, it is not necessarily "similar" to the home environment, but it is perceived as an enrichment experience.

Discipline offers still another perspective in scrutinizing the theme of continuity and/or discontinuity between home and day care. Most parents in this study feel that the way the center handles discipline is very similar to the way they themselves handle discipline, even though the center may do a somewhat better job of handling their children than they feel they accomplish at home.

Perhaps one way to examine the role of continuity is to consider the perception parents hold of the attributes of nurturance and warmth. This theme is expressed repeatedly but emerges explicitly when parents are asked what things they consider very, very important in the day care program. For instance, one program is in a crowded downtown area. This program offers a "free" tone, and when this researcher came to visit, several children, completely undressed, were having a wonderful time in sand and water. One parent who had chosen this program stated:

> The reason I chose the program he was in—how can I say it? . . . It had more of a new-age tone. . . . The people who had their children there seemed so similar to us and to have similar objectives in terms of their relationship to their children . . . and seemed more open to being concerned about their children's social life.

And another mother who had selected the same program commented:

> Margaret is such an amazing person that she colors the place so much. The place is run on her philosophy really . . . and I feel so comfortable with him being there because of that.

A parent who had chosen a particular infant center suggested:

> What a great place to be the first place. I was very lucky. . . . I felt like she was with another mother. They're just great. She could have been there until she was eighteen. I probably would have left her there.

A single mother who was raised in a family of six and found it initially very hard to put her child in day care comments on why she chose one of the family day care subsidized programs:

> I felt really good about the home situation. . . . It's like a family, like a mother and her little brood of six. . . . They go shopping in the grocery store together.

The emphasis on offering options and its concomitant connection to continuity between home and day care is a developing theme in this study. The importance of options has been suggested by Naisbitt in "Megatrends" (Naisbitt, 1982). States Naisbitt:

> The social upheavals of the late 1960s and the quieter changes of the 1970s, which spread 1960s values throughout much of traditional society, paved the way for the 1980s—a decade of unprecedented diversity. In a relatively short time, the unified mass society has fractionalized into many diverse groups of people with a wide array of differing tastes and values, which advertisers call a market-segmented, market-decentralized society (p. 260).

Offering options appears to be the most feasible way of achieving connectedness and continuity between home and day care, both for the parent and the child. Offering options is perhaps imperative in a culture where people now want and expect them. Offering options begins to address what Alison Clarke-Stewart states in her review of child development research as the need to develop a variety of programs for families "in different circumstances, with different cultural values" (Clarke-Stewart, 1977).

Bronfenbrenner has suggested the importance of looking at individuals within the total ecology (Bronfenbrenner, 1976). According to Bronfenbrenner, the microsystem is the immediate setting which contains the child, while the mesosystem encompasses the interrelationships between various immediate settings such as the child and day care or the child and school. The exosystem defines settings which do not directly contain the child, but do impinge on immediate settings in which the child functions, for example, day care and its relationship to the world of work (Belsky and Steinberg, 1978). One could argue that when families make choices, there is a greater likelihood that there will be a match between the microsystem and the mesosystem. Achievement of this match should facilitate a harmonious relationship between day care and the family.

VI

The World of Day Care —
An Enriched World or
a Less Than Optimal World?

I think it would be more negative for her not to be in day care. I'm pleased that she's there because I feel good about the center and now at this stage in her life . . . it's very much a positive influence to be with her peers.

(Stated by a single, divorced mother)

How do parents perceive the world of day care — as an enriched world or a less than optimal world? The parent's very perception of the day care experience may well set the tone for the child. Does the family enthusiastically venture forth into the day care setting, or is the utilization of day care perceived as something less than the best way to raise a child?

Researchers have studied what the effects of day care are on children. However, it is also important to know how parents perceive the day care experience. Do parents, for instance, believe that if the child is in day care they will not have the same influence over the child? In essence, we are asking, "If children are in day care, do parents perceive themselves to be as potent socializers of their children as if the children were not in day care?"

When parents were asked, "Some parents worry that if their child is in day care, they, the parent, will not have the same influence over their child, and other parents don't worry about this at all. How do you feel about this?" most parents expressed surprisingly little concern over whether they would remain as strong an influence over their children as if the children were not in day care. Over and over again parents commented that their influence was not lessened if their children were in day care. Parents perceived that the most important influence on their children is clearly the parental influence. In fact, thirty-six of the parents in this study are not concerned that their influence will be minimized. A single mother, in what she describes as a "pink collar job," discusses her preschooler:

> I've come to conclude that even though there may be influences during the day that I might not quite approve of, or they might be slightly different from the way I do things, I have concluded strongly that the influence at home is the strongest and always will be the strongest even though she's away from me nine hours a day. That's a long time for a little person . . . but regardless I still feel really strongly that just because the quality of interaction we have at home between mother and daughter—I don't really worry about the fact that my influence is going to be lost in the other hours of day care.

A student mother comments:

> No, I don't worry. I think that the influence that the parents have over the children is so big that if you can do something that can lessen it, it's good.

A married mother with an infant and a toddler, who is a teacher states:

> Not at all. I think one of the amazing things teaching older kids is that you realize the kids will have their parents' values. They won't have my values. I'm with them, you know, as a teacher of fourth graders, more hours than their parents are, but they still have their parents' values. The home is still the most important place. . . . The hours don't matter. The home is more important than any school or group situation.

However, parents perceive that it is the quality of the center which relates to the issue of influence. A mother who is a dietitian emphasizes:

> If he were at a place that I was unhappy about how it was being run or what he was being given, I might feel differently.

A married mother remarks:

> That's why I think it's important to pick a day care center that
> follows your philosophy and then it's not going to matter
> because the person who will be having influence will have the
> same influence, hopefully, that you would want them to.

And a single mother notes:

> Maybeck was special in that it was a little bit alternative. . . .
> Their values were similar enough to mine that I didn't feel any
> conflict. . . . If it had been a situation where the values were dif-
> ferent—very much different, then perhaps I would have [felt
> conflict], but perhaps I wouldn't have kept him there either.

When discussing the issue of influence, parents spontaneously bring up the subject of role modeling, an important
issue to parents. Children must have role models that parents
approve of. A single mother with one preschooler remarks:

> Maybe especially because I'm a single parent I want him to
> have significant others that are adults, so it's all right with me
> that there are other adults in his life that have an influence on
> him as long as their values are similar anyway. . . . They're very
> loving.

A married mother of two young children, a toddler and a
preschooler, emphasizes:

> They spend most of their time with you after all and you are
> their main . . . the parent is the main role model and actually if
> you go to the right place, like Muir, I don't think there's anybody
> there that I would feel bad if John were to model himself on.
> They're all good people.

And a single mother with one preschool son, who has chosen
family day care, notes when discussing the day care mother:

> Her philosophy about children is that we care about people,
> we're loving and we're kind, and that's her basic philosophy.

A single mother struggling to raise one child expresses the
opinion:

> They're [the staff] just incredible. They're really uncommon

people. . . . It's truly family connected, not just a custodial thing.

Interestingly enough, several parents mentioned that in center care where there is more than one adult, they were less likely to feel that their parental role was being taken over. Comments an unmarried mother with two small children, an infant and a preschooler:

I don't feel threatened by the center in feeling that they may move into my role. . . . That's one aspect to the group care where you have several adults rather than the one-on-one adult. I don't feel that any of them are trying to move into my role. If I had a situation that I was not comfortable with the people or the atmosphere or whatever, I think it would be different.

It must be mentioned that four of the parents in the study were concerned about day care influencing the child. Aggressive behavior is one fear expressed. An additional four of the parents in the study feel that full-time care is negative but part-time day care is not negative. It is interesting to note that these parents have selected part-time care. However, parents working full-time and utilizing day care full-time rarely mentioned the concern with full-time care.

One can also ascertain the extent to which day care is viewed as an enriched or less than optimal environment by examining the qualities parents believe their children have developed as a result of day care. This question obviously calls for speculation on the part of parents, since their children are in day care and it is difficult to ascertain what qualities are due to day care and what qualities are not due to day care. Parents have many thoughts, opinions, and ideas when they are asked if they feel their children would be different if they were not in day care. Parents were free to discuss positive or negative aspects of their children's development but approximately forty-three of the parents in the study spontaneously selected positive aspects to discuss.

Thirty of the parents in the study discussed the importance of social skills and the ability to operate within a group situation. Many parents believe that day care has facilitated and enhanced social development in their children. This belief is expressed in many ways by different parents. A single mother of a preschooler suggests:

> I think this [day care] is great for her social skills for one thing, and of course the sharing—that's real important to learn in life. And the giving and the dealing with different personalities . . . so I think she's getting an incredible education for her young life.

Another single mother suggests:

> It's [day care] very much a positive influence to be with her peers and . . . to learn how to interact socially and to share, and those kinds of things that if she were at home with me just on a one-on-one basis, the situations might not even come up if there weren't other kids around.

A married student mother notes:

> I think that the positive part is that [if he were not in day care] he would have been a lot more bored, maybe less socially secure. . . . His friendships are made through his child care center.

Independence emerges as another important quality that parents believe is facilitated by day care. Independence is viewed in a positive light. A married father who teaches, and who placed his son in infant care when he was several months old, suggests:

> He's a lot more independent now, but I think that day care's helped that independence—helped him know that he can be away from me and be all right and that there are other adults who can take care of him.

A working married mother with one preschooler states:

> I think he's more independent. There is a child that lives directly across from us who is three months older than Alex, who is much, much less independent—much less capable of standing up and playing with the other kids in the complex and always expecting mommy to intercede. . . . And Alex is a really tough little kid and I think he's got that from day care.

And a young student comments:

Independence is the first one that comes to mind. She's very independent and I would say if she stayed with us at home, I would be afraid that that would not happen because, well . . . I think we tend to overprotect sometimes because she's the only child also, and school—it's not like that.

Early learning is not one of the main themes which parents spontaneously discuss. In fact, only five parents bring this topic up. It is possible that parents assume early learning is taking place in the day care program. It is also possible that the theme of social skills is deemed more important and is more readily apparent.

Several of the parents in this study mentioned that there are negative aspects to day care. One of the perceived negative characteristics is aggression, and one parent definitely feels that her child is more aggressive because he does go to a day care center.

Parents in this study do not express significant factors that day care may adversely affect their children. The subject of the possible adverse effects of day care is, of course, one of the most salient issues in the day care literature, an issue about which researchers have extensively studied and professionals expressed a wide range of opinions (Blehar,1974; Cochran, 1977).

Parents also perceive the social realm of the child as an important positive area. Kagan, for instance, has suggested that children in day care might be more strongly influenced by peers than children not in day care (Kagan, 1972). However, parents perceive the social group as a positive influence which facilitates many, many social skills. One wonders if this positive perception of social skills expressed by parents in any way mediates the child's experience in the day care program? One also wonders how the child's readily developing social skills influence and reinforce the parent's positive perception.

Parents do perceive day care in a very positive context. In a sense parents feel that they have the best of both worlds—while they perceive themselves as the primary forces in their children's lives, they also perceive that their children are developing beneficial characteristics. It must, of course, be remembered that parents state that they have chosen a program consistent with their values. It is possible that if we once again think in terms of Bronfenbrenner's model, we are able to discern a harmonious interface between the microsystem and the mesosystem. This harmonious interface may well facilitate the positive perceptions on the part of parents.

VII

Day Care and the Subsidy

I do think that subsidies tend to bring together a larger range of social and economic backgrounds . . . and I think that's important. . . . When there's more money available [subsidy], there is more of a mix of families in different situations.

(Stated by a young subsidized parent)

In this northern California community, parents are free to use their subsidies at any of the CCC programs or any of the CCC subsidized day care center or day care home programs, providing an opening exists. However, subsidies are controlled, i.e., there is no center with almost all subsidized parents and only a few non-subsidized parents.

When the topic of the subsidy was introduced, many of the non-subsidized parents commented, "Oh, I don't know much about that." They were still asked their perceptions of the subsidy program. The subsidized parents, however, not only have a clear understanding of the subsidized programs, but express many opinions. Perhaps one of the most emotional parts of the interviews was when subsidy parents discussed the difference the subsidy made in their lives. A single mother notes:

Like if I had to make full board for Carol, it would be very, very difficult for me to make my rent plus her child care, plus my gas and food on the table and stuff. . . . (What would you do?) . . . I, well—like this lady I went to . . . she charged $1.25 an hour but it was gross. . . . In that situation I think you get what you pay for. And for me to leave Carol there, I don't know. I don't think I could have done it. . . . I don't know what I would have done, Becky.

And a student father with a toddler and a preschooler remarks:

We couldn't be at the Phoenix Center now, given our situation, if we didn't have a subsidy. So besides its being important personally, I do see where there's more money available, there's more a mix of families.

A young mother with two young children, an infant and a preschooler, who has recently separated from her husband, declares:

It's [the subsidy] just great for me. It's a blessing because I do have subsidy being a single parent. . . . My kids would not be able to go to CCC if they did not have subsidy.

One parent in the study did mention the relationship between the cost of his own taxes and the subsidy. He stated that the subsidy was fine as long as he didn't have to pay for it. (He wanted to make sure that his tuition would not be any higher because of the subsidy and that the subsidy money would come from other sources, not higher tuition on the part of non-subsidized parents.)

The subsidies, for many parents, meant the difference between not scraping by and actually having a chance to live with some dignity—pay the bills, put gas in their cars, and food on the table.

Because parents are encouraged to select any program available, they have a choice that would not be possible without the subsidy. In addition, as previously mentioned, the CCC organization encourages parents to make choices. Some parents become aware of options that they did not previously know existed.

When asking parents whether children should be exposed to various racial, social, and economic groups, the interviewer was very careful to state the question in a way that permitted parents to express a wide range of opinions. The interviewer said, "Some parents feel strongly that when their children are young, they want their children exposed to other racial, social, and economic groups and other parents are not so sure. How do you feel about this?"

Parents also appear to make their choice with confidence, since the CCC organization has carefully screened all programs. As one researcher has noted, many times parents do not really want a referral, but rather a recommendation (Levine, 1982). In a sense, the CCC organization is offering choice, but is also saying that the program has the CCC stamp of approval.

Thirty-five of the parents, both subsidized and non-subsidized, state that this is an important goal. Many parents express the view that knowing different types of people from childhood was important and related to the ability to get along with many kinds of people as an adult. Other parents comment on their own childhood, and some parents note that their limited exposure to other types of people was definitely a drawback in adult life. Still other parents connect exposure to many types of people with the issue of world peace. A young father who is not subsidized remarks:

> I think that [the subsidy] is a very important part of the program. I think that's a very valuable part of living in a community like this . . . and I think that's essentially what everyone needs to learn—is how to live with each other. The more variety that we have in terms of ethnic backgrounds . . . the more differences the kids are brought into—I think the more tolerant they will grow up to be.

A subsidized mother emphasizes:

> . . . That's a big part of it [the subsidy]. I grew up in San Francisco. There were Chinese and some blacks. . . . My parents brought us up to be not prejudiced at all and that's how I want Sally to be. I'm sure it helps a lot being around all different kinds of kids and stuff—different nationalities and races.

A single, subsidized mother struggling to raise one child comments:

> I hope I'm raising Carol really realistically, to know that there's really lovely people out there. It doesn't matter their income or their color or anything like that. And then there's real creeps out

there you have to look out for that are creepy for a whole list of reasons, but I think the more people and the more different backgrounds she meets in her lifetime and of course people from different countries, I think that's just going to make her a more well-rounded person—able to deal with life better.

And a single mother notes:

That was one of the points that drew me to Maybeck, in that it was racially mixed because that's hard to find too. . . . My family—we weren't exposed to people of other backgrounds—varied backgrounds—and I feel that I missed something.

Some parents are not sure about a racial, ethnic, and social mix. Four parents feel that having a diverse mix is not an important goal, and one parent feels that if diversity takes place and is given priority, standards might be lowered.

A major issue is not only what people think about subsidies, but what actually happens when subsidies are instituted. When both subsidized and non-subsidized parents were asked whether they felt that subsidies actually bring people together, subsidy parents are most apt to believe that this is true.

Thirty of the subsidized families state that subsidies do in fact bring different types of people together. Many non-subsidized families are unsure and are quick to point out that since the CCC system and the teachers are very careful not to discriminate in any way against subsidy families, they simply are unsure about who is and who is not on subsidy.

A divorced mother with one child comments:

That's the way I see it—that it brings different people together because at our center not everyone is subsidized by any means. I don't know the percentage of families that are subsidized. I don't have any idea, but I know that a lot of them pay full fee and so I think that's a plus for us. It brings different kinds of people together—those that are subsidized and those that pay full fee. It's a plus for her [the child] because the children she's exposed to at school are of varied backgrounds.

And a student remarks:

I think it [subsidies] brings ethnic yes, and racial yes [people]. . . . In thinking about the nursery school (a nursery school on campus), there are not subsidies there and the populations are from another group.

In contrast, five people in the study do not believe that subsidies bring people together.

Both subsidized and non-subsidized families believe that without the subsidy many families would not be eligible for the CCC day care programs because of the cost.

In some cases friendships or acquaintances are formed in the day care setting. Thirty-one of the subsidized parents report that either they or their children made friends because of the day care program. A mother with one preschool child comments:

> His friendships are made through the child care center. We carefully cultivated friendships with children. . . . This child care that he goes to, because it's part-time, is social and it's been a place to establish relationships with other parents with children the same age . . . and we do a lot of child care exchange.

A single mother with one preschool child remarks:

> Sure, I wouldn't have met these people—the ones in day care—for one thing, and I was thinking about that this morning as I was getting ready for work. The people I'm going to be introduced to in my life because of my daughter and her atmosphere. . . . Like tomorrow I'm going to go to a work party at Sierra and we're going to clean the roof.

Some parents are very busy and the friendships are more acquaintances. However, for other parents, friendships through school are indeed an important part of their lives.

Non-subsidy parents are much vaguer about the issue of friendships than are subsidy parents. However, non-subsidy parents mention once again that this is because they really do not know who does and who does not have a subsidy.

This study suggests that when parents have a subsidy, they are most able to choose a program with which they feel comfortable. The subsidy therefore creates an element of choice and control in the life of the parent. The parents venture forth positively in their search for day care because the programs are carefully monitored by the CCC organization.

This study also suggests that subsidies have a great potential for bringing people of various ethnic, racial, and social groups together. In a democratic society it can be argued that the possibility of different types of people coming together can create a type of cultural mix that ultimately enhances life in a democracy.

VIII

Day Care and the Quality of Family Life

I feel much better having my own sort of business — my own thing to do — and it's me. It's nothing I share with the rest of my family unless I choose to. And I really need to have something that I'm doing for me and . . . I think that I'm much happier and therefore my family is much happier with me working.

(Stated by a young professional mother)

In a society such as ours where the ethos of individualism is still woven into the American psyche, the concept of group care for children is always scrutinized carefully and critically. Day care, with its roots in day nurseries established during the Civil War, has long been associated with welfare. Nursery schools, or preschools, originating in the second decade of this century, were educational in nature, although they were not usually associated with the public schools. The increase in numbers of nursery schools, for the benefit of poor families during the Depression, followed by their conversion to child care centers during World War II for the children of working mothers, began to blur the original distinctions between day care and preschool. The question began to be asked and continues to be asked, "Should an educational component be included in day care?" (Almy, 1982).

But American society is changing rapidly. Daniel Yankelovich, as previously noted, discusses the Giant Plates of Culture (Yankelovich, 1981). As Yankelovich states, "The giant plates of culture have shifted drastically regarding the composition of American families. In the 1950s a working father, with a mother at home, and one or more children comprised 70 percent of American households. This norm has changed in one generation. Today it accounts for only 15 percent of the households. Single households have grown from 10.9 percent of all households in 1950 to 23 percent in the late 1970s" (Yankelovich, 1981).

Asserts Yankelovich:

> Most jobs are still organized as if these changes had not taken place. They continue to be full-time, five-day-a-week, regular hour jobs, with pay and fringe benefits based on the assumption that the jobholder is the sole earner in the family. We can expect vast changes in the future in how paid work and child care are organized. (1981)

The relationship between day care and the quality of family life must be examined within the context of the 1980s. Perhaps it can best be analyzed within our present cultural climate of relationships, work, and self-fulfillment. Yankelovich has suggested that approximately 80 percent of Americans are now committed to an ethic of self-fulfillment (Yankelovich, 1981). Self-fulfillment, for many families, is to be found in new roles, and for many women of childbearing age, the roles of parenthood and work are now combined. This cultural condition generates an urgent examination of child care and its relationship to family life.

It must, of course, also be recognized that many families who work must work. During the 1970s, the increase in single-parent families and escalating inflation contributed to the large number of mothers with young children who entered the labor force (Ruopp and Travers, 1982). The U.S. Department of Labor figures suggest that 25 percent of all working families with single parents would not have any earned income if they did not work. Forty-nine percent of working two-parent families would have incomes below $15,000 (1978) if the mother were not in the labor force.

When this researcher stated, "Some people feel that using day care and working or going to school makes life more enriching but other people disagree. How do you feel about this?" — most of the respondents said they want to continue working. Many of the respondents cannot imagine not working or being students. It is simply not within their experience. Thirty-five of the respondents find that having different roles is an important experience. Many respondents feel that their different roles benefit their families. A mother who is a teacher and who has a toddler comments:

> Well, I could never stay at home. I'd have to do something I think. . . . The days that I spend at home like vacation time—those are difficult days because I guess I'm just—I think Artie is just very demanding and if I were to stay home, I think he'd be demanding a lot. And I just have a hard time giving up so much of my time. . . . I look at my work, since I do like it, as something that's special to me and important and where I'm doing the things that I want to do. . . . Then I feel that I can give him that rest of my time, and if I stayed at home I'd feel much more pulled. I also feel that I would feel much more resentful staying at home.

An unmarried teacher who is the mother of a preschooler states:

> I feel it's probably the healthiest for both of us—being a single parent—because . . . I don't think I can provide as much as three teachers provide, three different people with three different approaches to life, or four teachers or however many he meets during the day. I also think after a certain point that I wouldn't be happy just being at home, so I'm happier if I'm doing work that I feel that I'm contributing to something other than just being a homebody. So I'm happier doing what I'm doing and then having our time together.

Some parents also wonder why parents should have to make a choice. A married mother comments:

> It is hard but I like it and I think that it's just crazy that women have to—if they have to choose between raising a family or having some work. . . . You have to have the two options at the same time—the two possibilities at the same time.

Some parents cannot imagine not working. A mother who is a writer and who has a toddler and a preschooler states:

> All people have a lot of roles. Nobody does just one thing or

another, so . . . once you decide to have children you have to assume the role of parent on top of everything else that you're doing. There's really no other way to do it. If really all you want to be is a parent, then I just think that would be really dull . . . if you dropped everything else just to turn into a parent.

And a single mother raising two young children, an infant and a preschooler, remarks:

To me it's really rewarding to work and to have kids.

A student mother comments:

I would go crazy if I were at home all day. I didn't know that but now I do.

Parents also feel the power of their own self-sufficiency. Comments a divorced mother with one preschooler who thought she would stay home for many years:

I like it very much [working]. I like what it's done for my life. It gives me a sense of self-sufficiency to do it and it means a lot, and comparing my life now versus what it was when I was home full-time—there will be times often when I'll say, I cannot possibly get out of bed this morning. I don't want to go to work. I want to stay home and have an extra cup of coffee. . . . But the trade-off for me of now having my own income, being responsible to no one else with what I do with my money—all of that part of it means a great deal to me and it's something that I would not change at all.

Many parents find that combining several roles is exhausting, but well worth the results. A single, divorced parent comments:

[Work and family]—A lot of times tiring . . . for all of us. Rush, rush, rush. Sometimes I get to a point if I have to do this one more day getting up at 5:30 . . . but on the other side of the coin I think I need the enrichment, the challenge of working and being with other adults in a work situation.

A mother who is a part-time teacher and has an infant and

a preschooler remarks:

> I love that job and I love being able to hold on to it but it's very tiring. . . . I find that it's just a drain.

Some parents however, find combining roles to be almost too much. Three parents find combining roles too tiring and one parent says, "Not enough time," while another parent says she feels a "conflict." An additional parent wishes she had more time "to be a parent" while still another parent longingly states, "This is not ideal. We work to survive."

When we examine day care and its relationship to the family within the context of the 1980s, it appears that many parents take the concept of self-fulfillment as their right. They want to be fulfilled and they expect to be fulfilled. Viewed in this context, high quality day care is an enhancing experience — enhancing precisely because it lets all members of the family have options. It is not just that day care permits a mother to work, but that it sustains and enhances the family's functioning in our present option-oriented society where many options are perceived not only as desirable but also as a right.

The findings in this chapter, in conjunction with the responses from Chapter IV, where most parents state that they see themselves as the primary socializers of their children and believe strongly that they as parents mainly influence them, argue strongly for day care as a positive influence both for the child and the family.

A phenomenon obviously does not exist in a vacuum. It occurs at a specific historical time within a specific culture. Cultural conditions with an emphasis on self-fulfillment combined with our current economic climate, put day care in a very different context than even ten years ago. These parents have a choice in the day care setting and are able to match their particular concept of what day care should be with the family's style and the needs of their own families.

However, it cannot be overemphasized that these parents are able to leave their children with ease because of the excellent day care situations. Had parents to choose among many poor day care programs, the same positive findings would most likely not have been forthcoming.

The sense of well-being that ensues and the sense of control parents feel may be viewed as the solution for the great day care puzzle. If one imagines that each piece has a focus, one could argue that parents are able to control the pieces and put their own day care situation together in their own way. Each family's puzzle looks a little bit different depending upon the needs of the family. What is important is that each family can design a puzzle that enhances its lifestyle.

IX

A Different Piece of the Puzzle —
The Directors' Perspectives

Parents have many perceptions, but what about directors? How do directors perceive the world of day care? Is their perception similar or dissimilar to the perception of parents?

Eight directors were interviewed. One director works in the administrative office and has an overview of the entire program. Five directors are involved in specific programs, with one of the five directing three infant care centers. Two individuals are day care home parents.

What Parents Want

When directors are asked what they feel parents are primarily looking for in a program, only one of the eight directors mentioned a structured program. Two directors mentioned safety, and the remaining directors discussed a program offering many rich activities and warm, caring staff.

A director of a program nestled in a suburban area comments:

Well, when they come here they're [parents] wanting a more open experience. Not a super-structured experience, but something—a place where I think the staff are going to watch their child and also stimulate them within that kind of structure so they're still learning. I think that they like this place because there's a lot of choices. Their kids can be indoors or outdoors all the time. They like that a lot.

A director of a center located in another section of town comments:

> I have a little section in my application that I always look at that gets at parent values. It's very brief and it's . . . but it's enough. All I do is have this little thing—this program input. It says, "After safety, what do you value and please rate them in importance." And most all of them rate number 1, warm and loving staff, and then they vary some. But basically you see the same three or four, sometimes in a little different order. They want materials; they want caring for their children first of all, almost all of them; they want facilities and toys; they want individual attention; and some put down discipline.

The director of a third center comments:

> Basically, in a nutshell, the philosophy is that our learning is pretty unstructured . . . that we set up the environment in a safe way and in an interesting way, and that the teachers are there to facilitate learning.

Several directors also mentioned that when parents come to visit their programs, they make it very clear as to what is and what is not being offered. One director operates a program based on a specific theory. She comments:

> One of the most important things of this theory is that—to look at the whole child and be concerned with every area of their development—their social, emotional, cognitive. And we don't put any one of those areas above any of the others. So a lot of people who have this strong desire to have their children pushed cognitively would hopefully be screened out by us in the very beginning. We would say, "We just will not do that. We're not going to teach pre-reading skills; we're not going to push your child to be reading by the time they leave here; we just won't do it. And if you really want that, you need to go somewhere else where the people at that school or that program feel good about doing that. We don't." And so, hopefully, we're usually pretty much in harmony with the parents.

Another director notes:

> They [parents] can be very different, but I like—I insist that when parents are going to come, that they have to stay with

their child here for at least an hour, watching their child . . . and seeing how we work with the children. I don't like to have parents come to our program unless they've had some experience and they feel really committed because I expect them to work with us. They must give two hours a month.

A home day care mother invites the parents in:

And I just—I invite the parent to come over for a first visit. I would tell them what a typical day would be like for their child in my home; what I would be doing. . . . I think I've evolved a pretty challenged day where I incorporate a little bit of everything they need.

Directors perceive that most parents want an enriched program with many choices and a warm, caring adult. Thus their perceptions parallel the responses made by the parents. It is also important to note that some directors make it very clear to parents as to what is and what is not being offered. This helps the parents make a very real choice based on adequate facts and information. This process also helps to screen out parents who might otherwise be unhappy with a specific program.

Day Care Homes

When directors are asked about day care homes, they have very definite opinions. Directors believe that many parents are fearful of day care homes.

The administrator who oversees both family day care and center care remarks:

Uppermost in everyone's mind is safety and the welfare and the well-being of the child. One reason is that day care has still a pretty bad reputation and every time there is—anything that happens in a day care home anywhere in the country, every day care home provider suffers for that. Anytime there is an abuse case or something happens, then parents naturally worry and we always get the backlash from that. I would like to have my child in a home atmosphere but I really worry about them being there—being alone there and isolated, and we don't know what's going on in the home. And I've heard so many horrible things happening, and how well do you monitor the homes? Could they do anything that they don't know about? How do you check them out? . . . They have also gross misconceptions about day care homes and centers, too, but mostly day care homes. They say, well, I don't just want someone who is going to be doing their housework all day; why not pay attention to my child. And what do they do with the children? And there's such an aura of mystery.

The director of a day care home comments:

In discussing the image that many parents hold of a typical day care home . . . the average day care home generally is a two-bedroom, thirty-year-old, ranch-style home with a small fenced yard . . . rather dingy. There's probably a dog or cat that's allowed everywhere in the house. The plumbing is old and all the rooms—the family room—they're all used for day care because there's not enough room to separate play areas from living rooms. . . . They may not necessarily like the children playing in their living rooms but because she has no other place, they have to play there. . . . I think when you pick up a magazine or newspaper or something and you think of an average day care home, that's sort of what people think about it. That's why we as day care providers have an image problem, if we choose to make it a problem.

The Subsidy

When directors are asked about the subsidy program, six of the directors believe that subsidies create diversity and bring different types of people together. This is said by different directors in different ways. A director of a lovely facility nestled in a large park-like area, comments:

Well, I think here, in particular, that people will come together, but there's a lot of choices here—a lot of places have different kinds of programs that are good. So they have a lot of real definite choices.

A director of a downtown center comments on how the subsidy has affected her program:

It has [created diversity] within my program. And the other thing, it has given me a much wider variety of people and values. . . . And the other thing that makes it interesting for everybody to work with and to be relating to each other, when you have those differences and values. And the other thing has been that all families get established and can then earn more because their child or children are in child care.

A family day care mother also stresses that in her program the subsidy has helped create diversity.

However, two directors feel that the subsidy does not create much diversity. One is a day care center director who believes ultimately that families come together based on values that are much like their own. The other is a day care home director who does not see the subsidy bringing people together. This finding is not easily explained but it is possible that diverse types of subsidy families have not selected these specific programs.

When asked about friendships between subsidy and non-subsidy families, an interesting finding emerges. Of the six directors who deal directly with parents (not including the two directors who monitor more than one program), three directors definitely feel that friendships take place because of the subsidy. However, two directors spontaneously bring up the division of friendship based on single versus married parents.

A director of a center in a low-income part of the city comments about friendships between subsidized and non-subsidized families:

Well, I think . . . they intermingle not according to subsidized or non-subsidized. I think more in terms of single-parent families and two-parent families.

The director of a small day care center located in a suburban part of the city, remarks:

I've found that the factor I think that seems to divide more—or be more divisive—was single parenting versus two-parent families. . . . I would have occasionally a single parent come to me and say, "How can we get some more support groups going? How can I talk to other parents who are single parents?'' . . . And I think that the needs and concerns of single parenting are unique.

The subject of friendship based on single versus married parents would be an excellent avenue for further research.

One day care home parent does not feel that subsidies help with friendships. She believes that subsidy parents are simply too tired at the end of the day to pursue friendships outside of her particular program.

Most directors assert that subsidy parents look at least at a minimum of two programs before selecting a particular program. Most directors are committed to the idea that parents should look at several day care programs in order to get a clear idea of the different types of programs that are offered. A director of a center program comments:

I think most of them have at least looked at two—at least, because, first of all, on their application they have a first choice, second choice, third choice. And everyone I've seen has always—all those three have been filled in.

The director who monitors all the centers and family day care home programs comments when asked about families making choices:

Yes. In fact, most of the centers and homes absolutely will not enroll a child or family without having interviewed both with the family alone and with the family and the child to make sure that everything is as they expected. Go over their policies with them; go over the contracts with them, and they say don't make a decision yet. Go see these others. Go see this one and go see that one. So we really not only encourage them, but we make it difficult for them to go to just one place.

One rather serendipitous finding emerged. While not one director of a center brought up any significant differences between the subsidized and non-subsidized parents, both home directors did bring up differences between subsidized and non-subsidized families. One day care home director said subsidized parents were "hostile," and a day care mother commented:

> What I'm trying to say is that a child whose mother is paying full fee, generally, I think, and I may be wrong when I think this, but generally she's able to provide for a better all around development of her child in economic, material terms. The mother who is not so well off, her mind somehow, her attention and her values about everything, always center on money because she doesn't have enough of it so she worries about her child's clothes, about his food, about all of those things and perhaps not so much about whether he gets applesauce today or whether he heard a story or whether he had music time.

Since this researcher had also interviewed the parent, she was aware that in one case the parent was very dissatisfied with the program, and in the other case the parent wanted to move his child into a center eventually. Do many parents not want family day care homes because of an image problem or are the day care home directors in some way projecting subtle messages to subsidized families?

Summary

In general, directors have very similar perceptions as those expressed by parents. Directors perceive that parents want a very rich program with a warm, loving staff. Directors also generally believe that the subsidy element of the program is very beneficial and does bring diverse types of families together.

Interviews with the directors also verify that from the administrative structure on down, parents are encouraged and expected to make choices. Directors try to make it very clear what specific components each program offers. This appears to help the parents greatly to make the choice with both understanding and clarity.

X

Choosing Day Care:
The Results of Alternatives

This researcher has studied one community with a variety of child care options. Many individuals have shared one part of their lives with this researcher—their definition of child care and how child care has intersected with their lives.

Fifty parents who had children either in the Community Child Care (CCC) day care centers or the private day care programs and family day care homes that have joined the CCC system were interviewed. Thirty-five parents received a subsidy and fifteen parents did not receive a subsidy. Parents were interviewed using a semi-structured open-ended interview. Eight day care directors and two family day care directors were also interviewed, using a semi-structured open-ended interview.

Findings of the Study

PARENTS WANT OPTIONS IN THEIR LIVES

Parents in this study expect to have many options in their lives. For most mothers the term "homemaker" is neither a term they use, nor a role in which they perceive themselves. Parents also expect to be "fulfilled."

Parents report that their own lifestyles have, in many cases, been influenced by their own parents. For the most part, their own parents do not disapprove of their grandchildren being in child care programs, and, in many cases, they view the use of child care programs as a positive experience. Grandparents have, in many cases, been delighted to see how their grandchildren have thrived in day care programs.

THE IMPORTANCE OF CHOICE

Parents in this city are offered many choices. Parents can choose family day care or center care. Parents can choose programs that vary in size as well as geographical location. Parents can choose programs that have a particular focus or philosophy. Parents can choose staff with whom they feel most comfortable. Parents have many choices, but because the whole system has been so carefully constructed, they are not able to choose poor child care.

PARENTS WANT PROGRAMS THAT ARE "WARM" AND "NURTURING"

Most parents make an arduous search for an excellent day care program. But what is it that parents are looking for? Overwhelmingly, parents are searching for a program that is "warm" and "nurturing." These concerns come up repeatedly as parents discuss what they want from any day care situation. The "feel" of the program and the "caring" of the staff are mentioned over and over.

CURRICULUM IS IMPORTANT

Program is important to parents and parents want just about everything—art, cooking, music, field trips, and science. Parents want these activities in a program that offers many choices throughout the day. Most parents do not want a highly structured program that emphasizes academics.

PARENTS SEEK HELP WITH DISCIPLINE

Parents report that discipline at the center is similar to their own but in many ways "better" than their own. Calm, patient discipline prevails at the center. Center staff explains and reasons with children, whereas parents may yell or, in moments of anger, "give a smack." Parents report that children are never ever hit at the center.

The center, in many instances, helps with discipline problems. Teachers at the center offer guidance, ideas, and support, which many parents appreciate.

FAMILY DAY CARE

Many parents in the study hesitate to place their children in family day care programs. These fears are often based on what they have heard about bizarre happenings at family day care programs in some cities. Parents also feel that center care offers a more enriched program. For the majority of parents, these are simply feelings since many parents have never visited family day care programs.

CCC

Parents rely on CCC for information about various day care options. In addition, parents express the feeling that if a program has been approved by CCC, they can enroll their children with confidence because CCC carefully monitors programs. Parents know that they themselves are expected to make the final day care selection.

DAY CARE—A WORLD OF CONTINUITY AND ENRICHMENT

Parents perceive the day care centers as offering both continuity and enrichment. Parents perceive the centers as extensions of their values and discipline techniques, but also as providing activities that they cannot provide. Parents do not view these activities—swimming, art, science, etc.—as discontinuous with home, but rather as enrichment activities that they view in a positive light.

Parents also believe that they have the same influence over their children whether or not their children are in day care. Parents view themselves as the primary socializers of their children.

Parents mention that they would be unhappy leaving their

children at the center if the staff at the centers were not competent. However, since almost all parents in the study view staff favorably, leaving children during the day does not appear to present difficulties.

Most parents express the thought that their children have developed positive qualities because they are in day care. The development of social skills and independence are two values mentioned most by parents.

DAY CARE AND THE SUBSIDY

Most parents, both subsidized and non-subsidized, believe that subsidies are a positive element in the program. Parents believe that subsidies provide an element of choice, create economic, social, and racial diversity, and bring different types of people together. Parents recognize that without the subsidy many families would not be eligible for quality day care.

DAY CARE AND FAMILY LIFE

Many parents express the view that the day care experience has helped them in their parenting and has helped their children in their development. They feel that day care has enhanced their family life.

VIEWS EXPRESSED BY THE DIRECTORS

The directors and family day care providers offer views very similar to those expressed by parents. Directors state that parents want a program offering many options, with a warm, caring staff. Directors also believe that subsidies bring people together and create the kind of diversity that would not be possible without the subsidies. Most directors state that parents look at a minimum of two programs. Directors make it very clear to parents what their particular program does and does not offer.

While the unique characteristics of the community and the Community Child Care's staff and programs limit generalizing the findings of this study to different communities, the findings do suggest factors that need consideration in planning for child care.

Implications of This Study

THE ADVANTAGES OF CHOICE

This study also suggests the advantages of having many types of child care in one community. Some programs are small (twelve or under), while other programs are larger. Some programs offer full-time care, while other programs offer part-time care. Some programs are in centers (in this study, decidedly the most popular form of child care), although family day care is also available.

When many types of child care are available, people feel they have a real choice. The mother who works until one o'clock in the afternoon does not necessarily need or want a program that goes until 5:30 P.M. or 6:00 P.M. She can choose a program that ends at 2:30 P.M. The parent who is a strong proponent of independent learning may want to select a program with that particular focus. Parents can create a match between their lifestyles and a particular program.

SUBSIDIES LEAD TO POSITIVE CHOICES

The subsidy program opens high quality day care up to people who could not otherwise afford high quality programs. It truly does bring different types of people together, particularly different income groups. In this study subsidies lead to choice, and choice from high quality day care options leads to parental satisfaction.

This study suggests that if a subsidy ever were to be instituted on a statewide basis, either for day care or the public schools, several aspects would need to be instituted to assure some mixing of ethnic and income groups and to further ensure that people select a program that most meets their needs: (1) a referral agency that could discuss the pros and cons of various programs and provide detailed information;

(2) programs screened for quality on specific agreed upon criteria; (3) a structure which ensures that a variety of income slots are allotted to each program. In other words, although there would be choice, all income groups could have access to each program. (4) Assurance that people could not add to their subsidies to get into certain programs. If one could add to his or her subsidy, it would undermine any element of choice for that segment of the population that could not financially add to its subsidies.

INFORMATION AND REFERRAL SYSTEMS

Information and referral systems — in this study, the CCC system — provide a vital function of "both providing important information and creating the best match between child care options and the needs of the family." Since CCC monitors programs, parents felt very safe in a program recommended by CCC.

Much recent day care literature has dealt with the Child Care Information and Referral agencies (Levine, 1982; Siegel and Lawrence, 1982). However, information and referral has its limitations. While some researchers have declared information and referral a major solution to day care problems, we must be wary about accepting information and referral as the total day care panacea. The information and referral system fits very nicely into the "less is more" philosophy and does solve many problems of hooking parents up with the best possible child care situation, but it does not solve the problem of families who cannot pay for good quality child care. "Less is more" only to a certain degree. After that point, less is clearly less.

EMPLOYER SPONSORED CHILD CARE

Some companies are now offering child care instead of another benefit such as health or dental care. This option is likely to increase, in part because in two-income families, spouses often duplicate benefits. Employers could do their workers a great service by having a child care referral agency and offering a subsidy to selected programs that have been approved. If the program studied serves as a model, approved programs should be selected and decided by professionals, with the help of parents, and that employees should only be permitted to use their subsidy at a list of approved centers or homes. This study suggests that parents who find excellent child care closely matched to their individual styles can feel a high degree of satisfaction.

THE ROLE OF PROFESSIONAL AND PARENT

In the field of child care and child development, parents have taken different roles at different times. Parents have ranged from participants in child care and nursery school to actual policymakers.

In this study the staff, who regard themselves as professionals, take a strong lead in the programs. They appear to take this lead with pride in their knowledge and skills. Just as doctors do not commonly ask patients which medication they would prefer, nor lawyers usually ask clients which law they would like the lawyer to focus upon, education has given skills and knowledge to those in the field and educators can go forth with assurance.

In this study parents report that the views of the teachers support and enhance their own parenting. This suggests that when teachers are well trained and work closely with parents, this expertise is most appreciated by parents. The center and home can work together creating a smooth interface between home and day care.

This finding is contrary to Powell (1978) who found a world of discontinuity between home and the day care center. Maintains Powell, "For many children it appears the boundaries of the child care center and family are sharply defined and narrow in intersection" (Powell, 1978). In the present study this was not the case.

The findings of this study also vary from Joffe's (1977). Joffe found that groups of parents in a three-hour parent nursery school program wanted different elements included in the program. One group of parents dominated the tone, while the other group dominated the curriculum.

Joffe's study suggests that participation is not always the key to an amicable relationship between parent and professional. Perhaps the reason that parents in the present study seemed more positive about the centers was because parents had an element of choice.

FAMILY DAY CARE

Kamerman and Kahn note that the demand for preschool in the three- to five-year-old age group is especially great and suggest that since this form of care is "costly" and "beyond the reach for many families," it is likely that the demand has not been satisfied (Kamerman and Kahn, 1979). Kamerman and Kahn's study raises the question of whether family day care would be the most utilized form of day care nationally if good quality centers were available.

Although nationally, family day care is the most utilized form of out of home care, this was not the preferred form of care in this study. The paucity of demand for family day care in the present study is possibly reinforced by several factors. First, the perception of family day care presented by the media cannot be underestimated. It was alluded to again and again by parents who had never visited family day care homes. Secondly, many parents perceive family day care as not offering the same quality programs as centers do, and parents want a program, not just "babysitting." This is not to say that family day care is just babysitting, but many parents perceive it as babysitting. If parents feel that family day care offers a program, they feel the program is not the same quality as center care where professionals, who are trained in child care, are in charge. Many parents say day care is providing a head start in life and they think this head start can best be nurtured by the professionals at a center. Finally, family day care, because it often accommodates a wide range of ages, may be more appropriate where there are two or more children in a family needing day care. This need appears to be declining as more and more families are having one or two children.

This study generates serious concerns about present state guidelines for low-income individuals who utilize day care. This researcher has visited day care centers in other cities where parents are neither required to pay a fee nor to make any contribution to the program, e.g., participating, work parties, additional repair and cleaning jobs that must be done to keep the center running smoothly.

In many of these centers, parents appear to have very little commitment to the centers. They drop the children off and pick the children up, but do not appear to have any ongoing commitment to the center.

Most of the families in this study appeared to feel great pride in their particular programs. Some parents do laundry while other parents attend work parties. Do parents who make a contribution feel a sense of "ownership" and concomitantly feel a greater sense of responsibility and community in the program? Paying a fee is still another matter. Since we live in a money economy, we must ask whether people value the day care program more when they pay for it. The issue of fees and responsibilities in a day care center should be considered by those who are deciding guidelines of day care funding for low-income individuals.

DEVELOPING A SENSE OF COMMUNITY

Questions of community are generated by this study. A high percentage of the respondents in this study expressed the feelings of close ties with their day care programs, which suggests a feeling of community. If parents are able to make choices and select a program that is comfortable for them, does a greater sense of community evolve? The development of a sense of community becomes an important issue in a society where people are struggling for supportive ties.

DAY CARE SUPPORTS FAMILIES

Finally, this study suggests ways that day care can support parental functions. First, parents have responsibilities in day care—both in fees and in working in the center. Secondly, teachers have a good understanding of child development and can help the family as developmental issues around child rearing evolve. Thirdly, since parents can make choices, they can select programs that most nearly match their parental styles. They can attempt to create some sense of community with other children and parents.

Within the model of Bronfenbrenner (1977), it can be cogently argued that day care is indeed a support to families. The individuals, the child and the family are supported in the microsystem which in turn is supported by the mesosystem. The mesosystem functions within a supportive exosystem—the Community Child Care (CCC) program.

Future Options

Where are we going as a society? How will we meet the needs of society's members? Certainly one factor we must consider is that of options. Not just the option to work or not to work, but basic structural options that would enhance family functioning. Shorter work hours, flex time, home employment, and job sharing could generate many changes in the quality of life for American families.

If these options were available, we could conceivably create changes in day care centers. There could possibly be more part-time preschool programs or day care centers with flexible hours.

The structure of day care in the future offers several possibilities. It is possible that day care centers might be under the public school system. There are both positive and negative aspects to the public school system having a large amount of money for day care centers. It is possible that day care programs could be made available to a wide range of income groups. Facilities and an administrative structure would most likely also be available under the public school system. If this administrative structure were sympathetic to early childhood and assured that individuals trained in early childhood were placed in the program, day care run by school districts might indeed work. However, one must also be wary.

On the negative side, teachers in unified school districts, who may not have had the appropriate training, could be placed in programs for young children. It is also possible that the public schools could opt for uniformity in curriculum and programs that can be measured, therefore potentially limiting choice.

It is also possible that money could be allocated on a county level and community groups could decide on the types of child care programs that are needed. While this possibility lends itself to the partisan political interests of various groups, and potentially to the involvement of individuals who have limited or no background in child development, it also lends itself to very positive possibilities. Individuals with excellent training in early childhood education could be recruited, and many diverse child care models might be created.

Finally, we as a society must grapple with the issue of affordable child care. We will end this study on a provocative thought offered by Gary Winget. Notes Winget:

> . . . The ultimate cost of unaffordable child care will be borne by our aging society three or four decades into the future; the failure to meet the needs of today's children will limit the potential of tomorrow's adults to support the social and economic institutions upon which larger and larger numbers of older Americans will be dependent (Winget, 1982, p. 357).

Appendix A: Parent Interview

Background Information

I am very interested in finding out about how you feel about day care, but first could you tell me a little bit about why your child is in day care? Do you work or are you a student?

Could you tell me something about your background? What did your parents do for a living? Did both your parents work and were you ever in day care or taken care of by a relative as a child?

So many things have changed in the last decade. I am interested in knowing when you were growing up, did you picture yourself as a working or student parent?

How do you find it working and raising a family?

If your parents are alive, do they have any feelings about your working and your child in day care?

Home–School Continuity and Parent Value Systems

Was it difficult or easy to put your child in day care? Were there pressures that said do this or don't do this?

What kind of activities do you feel should be going on in day care? Do you see these activities in your child's program?

Are these activities similar or different than the activities that you provide at home?

I am interested in how you feel that children should be disciplined. Could you tell me a little about how you discipline your child at home?

Could you tell me something about how you feel they handle discipline at school? Are you in agreement with it or have there ever been conflicts?

Sometimes a person's spouse or a person's parent disagrees about what type of day care is good for a child. Has this ever happened in your situation and how did you resolve it?

Have you ever been in a day care program that did not work out? Could you tell me something about it?

Sometimes parents worry that if their child is in day care they will not have the same influence over their child as if he or she were at home all the time. Do you ever feel this way?

I am interested in other ways that you think day care might affect your child. Do you think your child would be any different if he or she were at home all day and not in day care?

Some people feel that using day care and working or going to school makes life more enriching but other people disagree. How do you feel about this?

If you could plan any kind of day care, say center care, family care, or even a parent staying home and still receiving money, what do you think would be best?

The Relationship between Parent Values and Parent Choices

Could you tell me how you happened to choose this particular program?

Did you specifically want either family day care or center day care? Could you tell me about the differences you see between family day care and center care?

How did you hear about other programs?

Did you look at other programs?

Could you tell me anything about these other programs?

Did CCC provide any information which helped you choose this program?

Could you tell me some of the things that you consider very, very important in a day care program?

The Benefits or Lack of Benefits of the Subsidy and Integration through Subsidy[1]

Some people believe that subsidies bring people of different social, ethnic, and racial groups together in meaningful friendships. Other people do not believe that this is true. How do you feel about this?

---

[1]The word "subsidy" is used in this community.

Could you tell me something about the ways that you feel your child has or has not benefited from the program? What about yourself?

Would you be attending this program without the subsidy? What kind of arrangement would you have made if you did not have the subsidy?

Some people feel that children should be exposed to children from other social and economic groups when they are young and other people are not so sure. How do you feel about this?

Have you made any friends or developed relationships with people that you would not have met if it were not for the subsidy program? What about your child?

I am interested to know if your experience with subsidies will help you in selecting your child's formal school setting?

I thank you very much for participating in this interview. Is there information that I have not asked that you would like to tell me in order that I may fully understand the subsidy program?

Appendix B: Day Care Mother or Day Care Director Interview

Background

Could you tell me how you happened to become a day care mother (or day care director)?

Home–School Continuity and Parent Value Systems

Do you think there are ways that the world of day care and the world of the home are very similar or very different from each other? Could you tell me about these?

People sometimes want such different activities from a program. Some people want the three R's while others want a very free program with lots of free play. What activities do the parents in your program feel are important?

People have such different ways of disciplining children. Could you tell me some of the methods of discipline that parents in your program feel are important? Do you think the methods of discipline are mostly similar between home and school, or different?

Do you feel that most of the parents in your program — subsidy and non-subsidy — have child-rearing values that are similar or dissimilar to each other? Could you tell me about this?

The Relationship between Parent Values and Parent Choices

I realize parents come from many different backgrounds and may want different things emphasized in day care. But could you tell me some of the values and concerns about day care that most parents seem to hold?

I imagine at times there are real differences in what parents want from a day care program. Could you think of any examples of how one group of parents may have wanted one thing and another group something else and tell me how it was resolved?

Could you tell me some of the reasons you feel parents have chosen this program?

Do you feel that the parents who selected your program definitely wanted either family day care or center care and could you tell me about this?

Do you feel that most families with subsidies shop for several programs?

The Benefits or Lack of Benefits of the Subsidy and Integration through Subsidy

Some people believe that subsidies bring people of different social, ethnic, and racial groups together in meaningful friendships. Other people do not believe that this is true. How do you feel about this?

Do you feel that friendships between subsidy and non-subsidy children develop at school? Are they carried into the home setting?

What about friendships between subsidy and non-subsidy parents? Do they socialize and mix in and out of school?

Are there ways, other than economic, that you feel families are helped by the subsidy?

I thank you very much for participating in this interview. Is there information that I have not asked that you would like to tell me in order that I may fully understand the subsidy program?

Bibliography

ALMY, M. "Day Care and Early Childhood Education," in *Day Care: Scientific and Social Policy Issues.* E. F. Zigler and E. W. Gordon, eds. Boston: Auburn House, pp. 476–496 (1982).

AREEN, J. and C. Jencks. "Education Vouchers: A Proposal for Diversity and Choice," in *Educational Vouchers: Concepts and Controversies.* G. B. La Noue, ed. New York:Teachers College Press, pp. 49–57 (1972).

ARONS, S. "Equity, Options, and Vouchers," *Teachers College Record,* 72:337–363 (1971).

BECK, R. "Beyond the Stalemate in Child Care Public Policy," in *Day Care: Scientific and Social Policy Issues.* E. F. Zigler and E. W. Gordon, eds. Boston:Auburn House, pp. 307–337 (1982).

BELSKY, J. and L. D. Steinberg. "The Effects of Day Care: A Critical Review," *Child Development,* 49:929–949 (1978).

BLANK, H. "Child Care in the Year 2000," in *Current Issues in Day Care: Readings and Resources.* C. H. Thomas, ed. Phoenix:Oryx Press, pp. 11–13 (1986).

BLEHAR, M. "Anxious Attachment and Defensive Reactions Associated with Day Care," *Child Development,* 45:683–692 (1974).

BODENHAMER, G. *Back in Control: How to Get Your Child to Behave.* Englewood Cliffs, N.J.:Prentice Hall (1983).

BOOCOCK, S. S. "A Cross Cultural Analysis of the Child Care System," in *Current Topics in Early Childhood Education, Vol. 1.* L. G. Katz, ed. Norwood, N.J.:Ablex, pp. 71–103 (1978).

BRADBARD, M. and R. Endsley. "The Importance of Educating Parents to Be Discriminating Day Care Consumers," in *Advances in Early Childhood and Day Care. Vol. 1.* Greenwich:JAI Press, pp. 187–201 (1980).

BRONFENBRENNER, U. "Who Needs Parent Education?" *Teachers College Record,* 79:767–787 (1978).

BRONFENBRENNER, U., J. Belsky, and L. Steinberg. "Day Care in Context: An Ecological Perspective on Research and Public Policy," Washington,

97

D.C.:Department of Health, Education, and Welfare, ERIC Document Reproduction Service No. ED 157 637 (1977).

BRYDOLF, C. "Child Care Crisis: Bay Area Corporations, Government Team Up," *The Oakland Tribune* (July 27, 1987).

BRYDOLF, C. "Government's Growing Role in Child Care," *The Oakland Tribune* (July 27, 1987).

CATTERALL, B. and C. Williams. "Voucher Subsidized Child Care: The Hudson County Project," New Jersey State Department of Human Services, ERIC Document Reproduction Service No. ED 267 987 (1985).

CATTERALL, J. S. Education Vouchers, Fastback, Phi Delta Kappa Educational Foundation (1984).

CLARKE-STEWART, A. *Child Care In the Family: A Review of Research and Some Propositions for Policy.* New York:Academic Press (1977).

CLARKE-STEWART, A. *Day Care.* Cambridge:Harvard University Press (1982).

CLOW, S. L. "The Voucher Project, Final Report," Grant No. G-90-PD-10050, Salt Lake City, Utah:Phoenix Institute, ERIC Document Reproduction Service No. ED 272 319 (1984).

COCHRAN, M. "A Comparison of Group Day and Family Child Rearing Patterns in Sweden," *Child Development,* 48:702–707 (1977).

COHEN, D. and E. Farrar. "Power to Parents: The Story of Education Vouchers," *The Public Interest,* 48:72–97 (1977).

COONS, J. E. and S. D. Sugarman. *Education by Choice: The Case for Family Control.* Berkeley:University of California Press (1978).

COONS, J. E. "A Question of Access," *Independent School,* 44:9–20 (1985).

EMLEN, A. C. "Day Care for Whom?" in *Children and Decent People.* A. A. Schorr, ed. New York:Basic Books, pp. 87–112 (1974).

FEIN, G. G. and A. Clarke-Stewart. *Day Care in Context.* New York:John Wiley and Sons (1973).

FOWLER, W. and N. Khan. *Day Care and Its Effects on Early Development (Research in Education Series/8).* Ontario:University of Toronto, Ontario Institute for Studies in Education (1978).

FRIEDMAN, D. E. "The Challenge of Employer-Supported Child Care: Meeting Parent Needs," in *Current Topics in Early Childhood Education, Vol V.* Norwood, N.J.:Ablex, pp. 165–188 (1984).

GINOTT, H. *Between Parent and Child: New Solutions to Old Problems.* New York:MacMillan (1965).

GINZBERG, E. "The Economics of the Voucher System," *Teachers College Record,* 72:373–382 (1971).

GOLDEN, M., L. Rosenbluth, M. T. Grossi, H. J. Policare, H. Freeman, Jr., and M. Brownlee. *The New York City Infant Day Care Study.* New York, N.Y.:Medical and Health Research Association of New York City, Inc. (1978).

GRASER, R. "Employer Sponsored Child Care on the Rise," in *Current Issues in Day Care: Readings and Rresources,* C. H. Thomas, ed. Phoenix:Oryx Press, pp. 47–50 (1986).

HILL-SCOTT, K. *Child Care in the Black Community.* Los Angeles:University of California, School of Architecture and Urban Planning (1978).

HYMES, J. "Guidelines for Developing Legislation Creating or Expanding Programs for Young Children," *Young Children,* 42:43–45 (1987).

JESENIUS, C. L. and R. L. Shortlidge. "Dual Careers: A Longitudinal Study of Labor Market Experience of Women," Columbus:Ohio State University, Center for Human Resource Research, ERIC Document Reproduction Service No. ED 108 053 (1975).

JOFFE, C. E. *Friendly Intruders: Child Care Professionals and Family Life.* Berkeley: University of California Press (1977).

KAGAN, J. "About the Book," in *Day Care in Context.* G. G. Fein and A. Clarke-Stewart, eds. pp. xvii–xxi, New York:John Wiley and Sons (1973).

KAMERMAN, S. B. and A. J. Kahn. "The Day Care Debate: A Wider View," *The Public Interest,* 54:76–93 (1979).

KURZ, M., P. Robins and R. G. Spiegelman. "A Study of the Demand for Childcare by Working Mothers," SRI Projects URD-8750/1190), Menlo Park, CA:SRI International (1975).

LALLY, R., Jr. and A. S. Honig. "The Family Development Research Program," Syracuse, N.Y.:Syracuse University, Family Development Research Program (1977).

LA NOUE, G. R. "The Politics of Education," *Teachers College Record,* 73:304–319 (1971).

LARSON, M. A. "Federal Policy for Preschool Services: Assumptions and Evidence, Contract OEC-0-72-5016, Menlo Park, CA:SRI International (1975).

LASCH, C. *Haven in A Heartless World: The Family Besieged.* New York:Basic Books (1979).

LEVINE, J. A. "The Prospects and Dilemmas of Child Care," in *Day Care: Scientific and Social Policy Issues.* E. F. Zigler and E. W. Gordon, eds., Boston:Auburn House (1982).

LEWIS, A. C. "Education's Pro Choice Plan: If At First You Don't Succeed . . . ," Phi Delta Kappan, *Washington Report,* 67:331–332 (1986).

LOW, S. and P. G. Spindler. *Child Care Arrangements of Working Mothers in the U.S.* Children's Bureau Publication No. 46, Washington, D.C.:U.S. Government Printing Office (1986).

MAJTELES, D. "V is for Voucher, Valuable, Viable," *Day Care and Early Education,* 6:18–21 (1979).

MILLER, G. "Select Committee on Children, Youth and Families," *Families and Child Care: Improving the Options,* Washington, D.C.:U.S. Government Printing Office (1984).

MYERS, L. F. "The Family and Community Impact of Day Care: Preliminary Findings," Report No. PSU-CHSD-R-17, Harrisburg:Pennsylvania State University, Center for Human Services Development, ERIC Document Reproduction Service No. ED 097 096 (1972).

NAISBITT, J. *Megatrends: Ten New Directions Transforming Our Lives.* New York:Warner Books (1982).

NATHAN, J. "Shouldn't We Give Vouchers A Try?" *Learning,* 12:74–79 (1983).

PARDECK, J. T., J. A. Pardeck, and J. W. Murphy. "The Effects of Day Care: A Critical Analysis," *Early Childhood Developments and Care,* 27:419–435 (1986).

PETERS, D. L. "Day Care Homes: A Pennsylvania Profile," Report No. PSU-CHSD-R-18, Harrisburg: Pennsylvania State University, Pennsylvania State Department of Public Welfare, ERIC Document Reproduction Service No. ED 097 097 (1972).

POWELL, D. R. "The Interpersonal Relationship Between Parents and Caregivers in Day Care Settings," *American Journal of Orthopsychiatry,* 48:680–689 (1978).

POWELL, D. R. "Toward a Socioecological Perspective of Relations Between Parents and Child Care Programs," in *Advances in Early Education and Day Care, Vol. 1.* S. Kilmer, ed. Greenwich:JAI Press, pp. 203–226 (1980).

PRESCOTT, E. "Group and Family Day Care: A Comparative Assessment," Prepared for Family Day Care West: A Working Conference, Pasadena: Pacific Oaks College, ERIC Document Reproduction Service No. ED 060 945 (1972).

RODES, T. *National Consumer Study: Current Practices of Childcare Use in the United States, Vol. II.* Washington, D.C.:Unco, ERIC Document Reproduction Service No. ED 132 932 (1975).

RUBIN, L. *Worlds of Pain: Life in the Working Class Family.* New York:Basic Books (1976).

RUOPP, R. R. and J. Travers. "Janus Faces Day Care: Perspectives on Quality and Cost," in *Day Care: Scientific and Social Policy Issues.* E. F. Zigler and E. W. Gordon, eds. Boston:Auburn House, pp. 72–101 (1982).

RUTTER, M. E. "Socio-Emotional Consequences of Day Care for Preschool Children," in *Day Care: Scientific and Social Policy Issues.* E. F. Zigler and E. W. Gordon, eds. Boston:Auburn House, pp. 3–32 (1982).

SALE, J. S. "Family Day Care: One Alternative in the Delivery of Developmental Services in Early Childhood," *Journal of Orthopsychiatry,* 43:37–45 (1973).

SALE, J. S. "A Self Help Organization of Family Day Care Mothers as a Means of Quality Control," Presented at the 51st Annual Meeting of the American Orthopsychiatric Association, San Francisco, CA., ERIC Document Reproduction Service No. ED 094 306 (1974).

SIEGEL, P. and M. Lawrence. "Information, Referral and Resource

Centers," in *Making Day Care Better: Training, Evaluation, and the Process of Change.* J. T. Greeman and R. Fuqua, eds. New York:Teachers College Press, pp. 227–243 (1984).

STEINBERG, L. D. and C. Green. "Three Types of Day Care: Causes, Concerns, and Consequences," unpublished manuscript, Irvine:University of California Press (1978).

VERANZO-O'BRIEN, M., D. Leblanc, and C. Hennon. "Industry Related Day Care: Trends and Options," in *Current Issues in Day Care: Readings and Resources.* C. H. Thomas, ed. Phoenix:Oryx Press, pp. 42–46 (1986).

WALLIS, C. "The Childcare Dilemma," *Time,* pp. 54–60 (June 1987).

Westinghouse Learning Corporation and Westat Research, Inc. "Day Care Survey—1970," Washington, D.C.:U.S. Government Printing Office (1971).

WINGET, G. W. "The Dilemma of Affordable Child Care," in *Day Care: Scientific and Social Policy Issues.* E. F. Zigler and E. W. Gordon, eds., Boston:Auburn House, pp. 351–377 (1982).

WOOLSEY, S. H. "Pied Piper Politics and the Child Care Debate," in *The Family.* A. Rossi, J. Kagan, and T. K. Kareven, eds. New York:Norton, pp. 127–145 (1978).

WORTMAN, P. M. and R. G. St. Pierre. "The Educational Voucher Demonstration: A Secondary Analysis," *Education and Urban Society,* 9:471–491 (1977).

YANKELOVICH, D. *New Rules: Searching for Self-Fulfillment in A World Turned Upside Down.* New York:Random House (1981).

Young Children. "Public Policy Report," *Alliance for Better Child Care: ABC, V. 42,* pp. 31–33 (1987).

ZIGLER, E. F. and J. Goodman. "The Battle for Day Care in America: A View from the Trenches," in *Day Care: Scientific and Social Policy Issues.* E. F. Zigler and E. W. Gordon, eds. Boston: Auburn House.